COMPARITIVE DICTIONARY OF INDIAN AUSTROASIATIC LANGUAGES AND PUNJABI

Dr. Manzur Ejaz

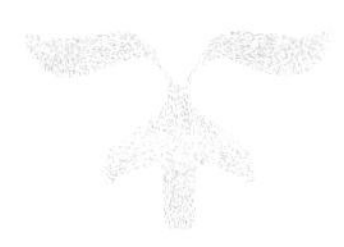

Acknowledgments

I am highly indebted to Dr. Jaspal Singh and Amandeep Singh who greatly helped me to complete this work. I also want to acknowledge A. Campbell, Manindra Bhusan Bahaduri, Nissor. U. Singh and Ronald Lee for using their Santhali, Mundri, Khasi and Romano dictionaries respectively. Without the help of these dictionaries such a project could not habeen envisioned.

Basic Key

C=ch

Ch=Sh

M=Munda

+M =Besides Santhali also in Munda

K=Khasi

+K= Besides Santhali also in Khasi

R=Roma (The language of European gypsies who migrated from Punjab)

+R= Besides Santhali also in Roma

--If none of the above given linguistic notation is given that means it is a Santhali word in column #1.

Note: This is part of an ongoing process and few words have not been confirmed. If you have any suggesstions in this regard, please send me a message on manzurejaz@yahoo.com

Santhali/Munda/Khasi/Roma	English	Punjabi
	A	
Aba (M)	Father	Aba
Abad	Cultivation	Abad
Abe tabe (M)	At the time	Aidon odon
Abgun	To injure oneself by over eating	Apharna
Abhagan (M)	Unfortunate	Abhagan
Abhola	Dumb	Bhola, bawla
Abla (M)	Feeble; helpless	
Abod (M)	Ignorant; young	Budho;
Abol	Weak	Abal
Abrak	Mica	Abrak
Abu (M)	We	Asin
Abua (M)	Our	Asada
Ac kathaae	That is as they say	Inj kehia
Ac	Himself	Uss
Achar (M)	Pickle	Acar
Achar	A heavy shower of rain	Achar
Achim	To sneeze	Acho
Achu (M)	To order; to ask; to command	Akhu
Achur (M)	To reach; to	Apar; upar

	arrive	
Acok (M) Achaka	Suddenly	Acanak; chanchak
Ad	The beginning	Ad
Ada adi	Not on speaking terms	Ada lana
Ada	To take cattle to mid-day resting place	Ada
Adai	To pay back	Adai; adaigi
Adalot	Court	Adalat
Adana (M)	Lowly	Adna
Adawa	Husking	Adawa
Adawati	Enmity	Adawat
Adda (K)	A stage for changing horses; dak-runner	Adda
Ade (M)	And	Ate
Adepase	Neighborhood	Asepase
Ader (M)	To take inside; to go in	Andar
Ader	To introduce	Ader (honor)
Adh	Half	Adh
Adha adhi	Half and half	Adhi adhi
Adha phada	Unfinished	Adha cadda
Adha	Half	Adha
Adhaia	Two and half	Adhia (half)
Adhela	A half price	
Adher	Past prime; getting old	Adhkar (Udher in Urdu)
Adhkhorca	Imperfect;	Adh pcad

	carelessly	
Adhuli	An 8 anna piece	Dhaili ; dheli
Adi; uttar	Much; many	Adi (from ad) (addicted in Urdu)
Adkar	One half	Adha; adhkar
Adkar; Adykar (K)	Thoughtfully; moderately	Adkar
Adol	Authority; right; jurisdiction	Adol
Adoli	To disregard order	Adoli (as in hukam adoli)
Ador	Pride; to sulk	Adar
Adra	To show temper; to be ill humored	Athra
Adwa	To husk	Adaona
Adwati (M)	Ill will; enmity	Adawat
Aedhori	To cultivate for half share	Adh te
Aedi	To whine	Ooi
Aema	Many	Aam
Aere	To deviate; to swerve; to diverge out of direct course	Aere (like in aere gaere)
Agad	Increase the size	Agga
Agam (M)	Future	Agam
Agam	Future	Age
Agar (M)	If	Agar; jekar
Agardigar (M)	Forward and	Agepiche

	backward	
Agdhao	Postpone	Agge wadhao
Ager	Heavy in front as loaded cart	Ager
Ages (R)	Today	Aj
Agil	Heavy in front	Agar (opposite of alar or ular)
Aglaha	A leader; who goes before	Agla
Agotar (M)	Rent or payment given in advance	Agotar; pashgi
Agu; au (M)	To bring	Liao
Aha (M)	Alas	Afsoos
Ahh uhh	Cry of pain	Ahh uhh
Ahil mahil	To delay; to put off time	Ahlak
Ai-bud-nam (K)	Slander; to defame	Badnam
Ai-kai (K)	To give for a time; to pretend to give	Kai
Ai-ksuid (K)	To kill or bring disease to a person by the agency of devils	Kuhna; kusna
Ai-li; Ai-mon (k)	To give one his own way	Leeh
Ai-pop (K)	To charge with; to blame for	Pap
Ai-ronge (K)	A paint	Rang

Ai-sakhi (K)	To give evidence	Sakhi
Ai-shah (K)	To give on credit	Shaukar
Ai-sut (K)	To give money on credit	Sod
Aice	Come	Aao
Aidari	Possession; authority	Amaldari
Ain (+M)	Law; statute	Aein
Ainthao	Twist	Ainthana
Aja	Grandfather	Dada
Ajait (M)	Outcaste	A-zat (zaton bahar)
Ajan	Ignorant; without knowledge	Ajan; anjan
Ajbajao (M)	Entangle	Arao; uljhao
Ajgar (M)	Powerful; vast	Ajgar (comes to describe powerful snake)
Ajhal pajhal	More than enough; unlimited	Ajhal (used with knowledge; preacher)
Aji (M)	Grandmother	Dadi
Ajmae; Parikha;Imtihan	Examine	Ajmana;Parikha;Imitihan
Ajmao (M)	To examine	Azmao
Ajmao	To examine	Azmao
Ak	Sugar cane	Ag (upper green part of sugar cane)
Ak; Aku (K)	Expressing disgust at a bad smell	Akhu

Aka	To hang; suspend	Atkaona
Akabaka (+M)	To be surprised; to be confused	Hakabaka
Akabaka	Very quickly; rapidly	Akabaka ; cancak
Akaj	Useless	Akaj (opposite of kaj; kam)
Akal (M)	Famine; scarcity	Kal
Akal	Famine; dearth; scarcity	Kal
Akal	Famine	Akal
Akath (M)	Unspeakable	A-kath (na kahi jan wali)
Akathar (R)	From here	Aidron; aithon
Akhar bakhar	At random; thoughtless	Akar bakar
Akhara (M)	A place for dancing or meeting in a village	Akhara (more used for wrestling place)
Akharal (R)	Call; invite; summon	Akhia
Akhir (M)	End	Akhir
Akhir(K)	Domesday	Akhir; akheer
Akhir;Khatam	End	Akhir;Khatam
Akhor	A letter of the alphabet	Akhar
Akhrot	Walnut	Akhrot
Akka Bakka	Distressed	Hakka Bakka
Aktear (M)	Power; control; authority	Akhtiar

Akul bakul	Confounded	Be-aqli
Alacar	Helpless	Lacar
Alae-balae (M)	Misfortune; misery; to be in trouble	Alae-balae
Alag balag	Wide apart; various	Alag thalag
Alag	Separated	Alag
Alam galam	Indistinctly	Alam galam
Alan (M) Alang	The tongue	Alawna; bolna
Alang (M)	Tongue	Alaw'na
Alaria	To wish to be fondled or taken up in the arms as a child	Ularna
Alau	Ignoramus; Simpleton	Yalah; ala-bhola
Alav (R)	Word	Akhar; alawana
Albat salbat	Contradictory	Ala bla
Ale (R)	Here	Ale; ethe
Alekha	Which cannot be assigned number	Alekha (opposite lekha)
Almal	Confused	Dhilmil
Alu (M)	Potato	Alu
Am-saphri (M)	Guava	Amrud
Amali; amla; amoli	Authority; office; title	Amal; hakim
Amanat (M)	To deposit; in someone's safeguard	Amanat
Amanot	To give in trust	Amanat
Amaro (R)	Our; ours	Hamaro; asada
Amas (M)	New moon	Amas

Amber	A tree	Amber
Amda; amdani (M)	To be in possession; income	Amda; amdani
Amdaj	Conjucture	Andaja
Amdani (M)	Income	Amadni
Amdani	Income	Amdani
Amela	Abundant; unlimited; great in quantity or number	Ugla (Iknan ata ugla; Farid)
Ami (R)	We	Asin
Amin	Amen; let it be	Amin
Amla (M)	Office of a court	Amla
Amol	Time	Origin of mamol
Amrud (M) Am-saphri	The guava	Amrud
Amsi (+M)	Mango dried in the sun	Amsi
An (M) Ain	A privative prefix like English in un	An (like in Anhoni)
An (R)	To see	Annah; as blind; seems to be originated from this
An	A law; an enactment	Aeen
An	Understanding	Aona (of something)
An-dhan (M)	Wealth	An-dhan
An-hos (M)	Unconsciousness	Ah-hosh; behosh
An-hut (M)	Many	An-hut

An-katha	Unspeakable	An-katha
An-pach (M)	Indigestion	An-pac
An-pani (M)	Food and drink	An-pani
An; anaj (M)	Wheat; grain	An; anaj
Ana gona	Come and go	Ana jana
Anachu (M)	The act of sneezing	Uchu lagna
Anaj (M)	Grain	Anaj
Ananas	The pine apple	Ananas
Anar	pomegranate	anar
Anari (M)	A newcomer; inexperienced	Anari
Anav (R)	Name	Nan
Anbhul; anthul	Unconscious	Anbhul
Anbid	Immeasurable	Anbid; behad
And (R); andar; ande	In; into; inside	Andar
Anda dhund (M)	Exceedingly; furiously	Anda dhund
Anda manda	To go aimlessly	Anda janda
Anda-a (M)	To fry	Anda (egg)
Ande sare thana	In all paces; everywhere	Andar sare than
Ander ondor (M)	To walk aimlessly	Aidhar udhar
Andesara (R)	Evening; dusk; nightfall	Andhera; hanera
Andge	Testicles	Ande; tatte
Andha (M)	Blind	Anha; andha
Andha dhund (M)	Greatly;	Andha dhund

	severely	
Andha	To blunder; by mistake	Andha
Andhar	Darkness	Andhir
Andher (M)	Unjust; unlawful	Andher; haner
Andhi (M)	Blind (female)	Andhi; anhi
Andhi dak	A storm of wind and rain	Meenh hanari
Andhi	Wind storm	Andhi
Andhkup (M)	Great darkness	Ghup hanera
Andhri (M) Andhi	Blind female	Annhi
Andhru	Blind male	Annha
Andhua; rat kana	Night-blind; half blind; nearly blind	
Ando (R)	During; in; inside	Andre
Ando than (R)	In place of; instead of	Ais than
Ando wast (R)	In hand; in one’s possession; under one’s ownership	Hath wast; hath wich
Andra (M)	Ignorant; stupid	Andra; anha
Andra	Not effectually castrated	Andra (the testicles are called anda)
Andu (M)	Leg ornament	
Aneao (M) Aneae	Injustice	Aneao
Aneao (M)	Unjust;	Aneao; anea

	injustice	
Anel (R)	Bring; carry; deliver; fetch	Ana lia
Ang (M)	To dawn	
Anga (M)	Dress; coat	Angia (derivation)
Angao (M)	To wish; to desire	Tahng; amang
Angar (R)	Coal	Angar
Angen	To disappear	Angen
Angikar;Manjur	Accept	Manjur
Angla; angle (R)	In front of; ahead of; preceding	Agla
Angraji	English	Angrazi
Angrushti; angushtri (R)	Ring	Angothi; angushtri
Angur	A grape	Angur
Anhos (M)	Unconscious	Anhos; behosh
Anhut (M)	Independent; many	
Ani; hani	Injured	Root for hatia
Anja	Grain	
Anjan (M)	Ignorant	Anjan
Anjan	To blacken and improve eyelashes	
Anjante	By mistake	Anjane
Anjanti (M)	By mistake	Anjane
Anjir	The pear shaped guava	Anjir
Anjir	The pear shaped guava	Anjir
Ankarwa	Unable to control	
Ankur (M)	To	Anguri (Zakham

	germinate; new buds from seeds	te angur awna)
Ankus	A hook; an elephant goad	Ankus
Anman (M) Anuman	Guess; inference	Anman
Anman	Temporarily; for the time being; meanwhile	Anman
Anna (K)	Idiotic	Anna; jhala
Antar (M)	Measure of the distance between one furrow and another; made while ploughing the field	Siarh
Anthari	Out of place; anywhere	Anthari (who doesn't have thar or place)
Antra (K)	Chorus	Antra
Anu anu	Of many kind	Be-ant
Anuman (M)	Exactly	Anuman; hu-behu
Anumi	Deliberately; on purpose; purposely	Manun; man ton
Aoaj (M)	Sound; noise	Awaj; awaz
Aoal	First; best	Awal; pahla
Aosan (+M)	To make easy; to lighten;	Asan

	leisure	
Aosan	Ease	Asan
Aotha	A ring worn on the great toe	Angotha
Apai	Fault; transgression; sin	Apai
Apaj	To urge each others to do things and waste time	Apaj (Paj meaning excuse)
Ape (M)	More than two	Ape
Ape	You	Ape; Ap
Ape-ke (M)	To you all	Apke
Apepase (M)	Near about; close to	Asepase; aledwale
Aphil	Appeal	Appeal
Aphim (M) (K)	Opium	Aphim
Aphim (M)	Opium	Aphim
Aphoti	Calamity; distress	Aphat; afat
Aphsor	Opportunity; leisure	Aphsor
Aphsor; opsor	Leisure	Afsar
Apil (M)	Appeal	Apil
Apna apni	Everyone for their self	Apo api; apa dhapi
Apnao (M)	To come to onself	Apnao (to own)
Apnao (M)	To own; to make one's own	Apnao
Apod	Trouble; calamity	Pawara

Apradi	Criminal	Apradhi
Apre	My	Apna
Apsoch (M)	Regret	Afsoos
Aptar	To be untidy; to be littered; to be dirty	Abtar
Apus (M)	Relations	Apus
Aqil (M)	Wise	Aqil
Aqil Gawar	Foolish	Gawar
Ar (M)	And; or; other	Hor; aur
Ar	More; in addition to	Aur; hor
Ara (M)	A big saw	Ara
Ara	Spoke of wheel	Ara
Ara	Spoke of wheel	
Araj (M)	Prayer; petition	Araz; araj
Arak	Pot herbs; vegetables	Arak (juice)
Aran	Cry	Aran; arana
Arana (M)	Yoke of the plough	Jula (but the shuttle stick that keeps bullocks' neck inside are called 'arlian' which is derived from arana)
Arandi (M)	Marriage arrangements	Arnbhna
Aranga	Large; enormous	Aranga
Arao (M)	To be	Arial; aridar

	disobedient; lazy; obstinate	
Arar	A yoke; To accept responsibility	Arar (Arli derivation)
Arar	Yoke	Arli (derived from this root)
Arath (M)	Meaning	Arath
Arc pase	Neighborhood; vicinity	Ase pase
Arda (+M)	In a state of nature; fallow; unbroken; to work; uninured; time; span of life	Arda
Ardas (M)	Hope	Ardas
Ardas	To complain	Arzi
Are	Edge; margin	Kinare
Argat	Proper time; favorable time; in good time; morning; early	Argat
Arho	Again; more	Hor; ahar
Ari (M)	To bellow (used of buffalos only)	Aringna
Ari	A hand saw	Ari
Arja arjhi	Request; excuse	Arzi
Arja	petition	Arja

Arjao	To gain; acquire; to obtain a good harvest or crop	Jhar (per acre yield)
Arjon	Agricultural produce; crop	
Arkha (M)	To covet; to wish what another has got	Hirakh
Arkhap (K)	Cleft; place beween two up-rising mounds	Khapa
Arkup	Two suits of cloths	Kapra (kup is kapra and ar is 2 in Khasi)
Aroj (M) Arji	Request; petition	Arz
Aront (M) Arant	A warrant	Warrant
Arosi parosi (M)	Neighbor	Arosi parosi
Arosi parosi	Neighborhood	Aros paros; gwandh
Arot (M) Arath	Meaning	Arth
Arra (M) Ari	To bellow	Arana ; aringna
Arrao	To below	Arrao (like cow or buffalo)
Arsi (M)	Mirror	Arsi
Arsi	Mirror	Arsi
Arti (M)	Hearse	Arthi
As (M)	Hope (M) Turn; time; chance	As
As (M)	Turn; time;	As (hope)

	chance	
As	Expect	Aas
As-bharosa (M)	Hope	AS-bharosa
Asa jawa	Coming and going	Aona jana
Asal (M)	Principal; chief; pure; true	Asal
Asami (M)	Tenant; opposite party in a law suit	Asami
Asami	Client	Asami
Asarphi (M)	Golden coin	Ashrfi
Asat (M) Asathi	False; untrue	Asat (opposite sat)
Asat	Untrue	Asat
Asathi (+M)	False; unfair	Asathi (opposite of sat; thetruth)
Asawaria	A rider	Aswar
Asbab (K)	Luggage	Asbab
Asen	To conduct; to tend	Asen
Asepase (M)	Around	Asepase
Asirbad (M)	Blessings	Ashirbad
Asis	Curse	Asis
Askat	To be lazy; indolent; sluggish	Ahalki
Asnan (M)	Bath	Ashnan
Asol (M)	Chief; fundamental; real	Asol
Asol	Genuine	Asli
Aspas	Neighbourhood	Asepase

Asra (M)	To hope; to expect	Asra
Asra	Support	Asra
Asrae (M)	A shelter; a refuge	Sarae
Asrat	Old and large	Asrat (the effects)
Astabal	A stable	Astabal
Astin (M)	Sleeve	Astin (Urdu)
Astir (M)	Patient; calm	Asthar
Asto ghari	Always; all the day along	Har ghari; ik ik ghari
Asul (+M)	To maintain; to nourish	Asul
Aswar;aswari	riding;act of	aswar;aswari
Aswari; Sowari	Riding	Aswar; swar; swari
At (K)	To swell to; to bulge out; to harbor ill feelings	At; at chukna
At patao	Confused	At pata
At sat	Contradictory	Ata sata
At	Intense	At
Ata (+M)	Flour	Ata
Ata (M)	Flour	Ata
Ata	A raised platform from which wild animals are shot; an ambush	Ata
Ata sata	Food	Ata ota
Ata	Flour	Ata
Ata-ati (M)	To quarrel; to dispute; to	It-vatta

	argue	
Ata-sata (M)	Close together	Ata-sata (to exchange equally)
Atal	A layer; story; row upon row	Tal
Atarde (R)	Hither; here	Aidar
Ate (M)	With; by means of	Ate; ute
Aten	To listen; to-eavesdrop	Aten (confidants)
Atha	Unfathomable	Athah
Athah (+M)	Bottomless; very deep	Athah
Athah; athan (M) Atha	Bottomless; infinite	Athah
Athre	To place under for purpose of raising; to rest on; to put in wedge	Athra
Athwara (M)	Eight days; a weak	Athwara
Ati (M)	Bundle; sheaf	Ati
Atiar (K)	Instrument; weapon	Hathiar
Atit	To leave home and become jogi	Atit
Atkao (M)	To prevent; to stop	Atkao; atak
Atkao; atak (M)	To prevent; hinder	Atak; atkana

Atkura	Childless; barren	Untra nkhatra
Atma (M)	Spirit	Atma
Ato	A village	Ato
Atok; Atkao; Atok	To obstruct; to prevent	Atkana; hutak
Atom	All; everyone	Atom; tamam
Ator	Sweet scent	Atar
Atpatao (M)	To struggle; to be restless	Atpatao
Atra	To fail; to come short	Atar (ajaz)
Atrom atrom	Half; incomplete	Adh-pacada
Atut bir	Dense; primeval forest	Atut bar (jungle)
Atut	Many; very many	Atut
Atweto (R)	Answer; reply	Itwata
Au	An interjection of surprise	Au; hau
Aual (M)	First; pure; best	Awal
Aujhar	To entangle; occupied	Aujhar
Aukhan	Dangerous	Aukha ; mushkal
Aulau	To confuse	Walau
Aura (M)	A kind of fruit	Aru
Ausan	To get relief from grief	Ausan
Ava (R)	Yes	Aahu
Avel (R)	Attend; be coming; come	Aa (avel will be come again)

Aver (R)	Other; another	Hor
Aver nav (R)	Alias	Hor nan
Aver-tehara (R)	The day after tomorrow	Hor dehara
Aver-than (R)	Elsewhere; somewhere else	Hor than
Aver-zheno (R)	Another person; somebody else	Hor jana
Avlin (R)	Mansion; manor; palace	Havali
Awa (M)	A potter's kin	Awa
Awa; Awali	Spokes of a charkha	Awali
Awaj (M) (K) Aeoaj; awaj	Sound	Awaz
Awal (M) Aual	First	Awal
Awria (K)	Licentious	Awara
Ayo (M)	Mother	Man; mao (Aye di sonh; Shah Hussain)
Azhukerel (R)	Wait; wait for	Udek
A~bole	Said	Bolia
A~c	Fire	A~c; ag
	B	
Ba (K)	That; for; since	Ba
Ba kobi	Cauliflower	Gobhi
Ba	No; not	Ba (babghair etc)
Ba-iho (K)	Fear	Bho
Baahca; caro	To hire Bullocks for	

	agricultural purposes for a year	
Bab	A cess imposed by feudal	Bab
Baba (R)	Old woman; old witch	Budhi
Baba	Grandfather	Baba
Babai; ba-bai-ko (M)	To repair; builders	Banwai
Babat (M) Babta	To itch	
Babha (K)	Good	Bhala
Babla	The name of a tree	Babol; kikar
Babna (M)	A dwarf	Bona
Babroshi	A cook	Bawarchi
Babu (+M)	A boy; a son; a way to address	Babu
Babu (K)	Baboo; a writer; a school master	Babu
Bac	To deliver	Bac (bach; lagan &c.)
Baca	Answer from a witch doctor; to find out	Baca (Promise; Bani kar ke)
Bacalo (M) Bachao; babchao	To preserve; to save	Bacao
Bacao	Defend	Bachana
Bacha	Calf	Bacha
Bachha (M)	A bull calf	Wacha; baca
Bachhi (M)	A female calf	Wachi; bachi

Bachra	Colt	Bachhera
Backar	A prostitute	Badkar
Bacol	To escape; salvation	Baca
Bacra	Immature; young	Bacra (baby)
Bad (M)	To subtract; to increase; flood	Bad; baad
Bad	After; afterwards	Baad
Bada	A loan of seed given at sowing time for which a double quantity is returned at harvest	
Badac	To know; to be cognizant	Wac
Badai (M)	To be vain; glorious	Badai
Badalte	On account of; with a desire to injure	Badla lena
Badam	Almond	Badam
Badao	Ill will; hatred	Badi
Badaria; badgaria	Fastidious	Bad-kar; bad-damag; Bdaia
Badbad	Bubble	Bulbula
Baden	An irrigated rice field	Bhoein
Badha	Wooden sandals	

Badhao	Enlarge	Badhao
Badhao; badhaona	To increase	Wadhao
Badhi	To bandage; to join	Badhi
Badhoe; badohi	A carpenter; a wool worker	Brahi
Badhona	Increase	Badhona
Badhoria	Expert in working in wool	
Badi (M)	Enemity; ill will	Badi
Badi	Large quantity	Badi; buht
Badil (R)	Annoy; bother; disturb	Bad-dil
Badla (M)	Revenge	Badla
Badli		To exchange
Badmos	scoundrel	badmash
Badnam	To disgrace; to give a bad name to	Badnam
Badot	To be at enmity; to bear a grudge; to bear ill	Badot (badi te aona)
Bae; bana-e	Not; without	Bae; Bana
Baela	Tall; long	Baela (buhta lama)
Baena (M)	Earnest money	Baena
Bag	A bridal	Wag; bag
Bag;Lagam	Bit (horse's)	Bag; Lagam

Bagan (M)	A garden	Bag
Bagdao	To destroy; to go wrong; to be spoiled	Bagrao (wigar gia)
Baghar (M) Bagahi	Dangerous; infested with wild animals	Baghar (like in baghar billa)
Bagi (M)	A tumtum; a cart	Bagi
Bagi	to quit	bagi
Bagicha (M)	Garden	Bagicha
Baglotte	Unintentionally	Basoce
Bagor;Bin	Without	Begar;Bin
Bagrao (M)	To spoil	Bagrao
Baguli (M)	A purse; a pouch	Bagci; bagli
Bagwan	Garden care taker	Bagwan; mali
Bah (K)	An elder brother; to carry on one's back	Bah; bhar
Bah bah (+M)	Bravo	Wah wah
Baha	The monthly courses of women; menses; the placents	Mahwari; waha (from wahan as of blood)
Bahaj	Without	Bhaj
Bahal (M)	To engage; too much liberty to a child	Bahal (reinstate)
Bahalao; bahali	To comfort; to sooth	Bahlao

Bahali (M)	Appointment	Bahali (reinstatement)
Bahana (M)	Excuse	Bahana
Bahar	External	Bahar
Bahar; Baher (M)	Outside	Baher
Bahi (M)	An accountant book	Wahi
Bahi	A heap; a pile; large quantity	Bahi (buhti)
Bahi	Arm	Banh
Bahka	stray	bahka
Bahkao (M)	To attempt to allure	Bahkao
Bahlao (M)	To amuse	Bahlao
Bahni	A whirl pool	
Bahonhar	Brother-in-law	Bahanwaia
Bahra (M) Bahira	Deaf	Bola
Bahra	Deaf	Behra
Bahu	A bride; a wife (M) Younger brother's wife	Budhi; wohti; tewin; zal
Bahu	Bride	Bahu
Bahula; bahli; baulaha; baulahi	Insane; crazy	Bawala; Bawali
Bai (M)	To make; to prepare; to build; to create	Banai
Bai (R)	Surely; so	Bae
Baibaite (M)	Carefully	Baibaite
Baid (K)	Peevishly	Bhaid

Baida; (+M) baid	Doctor of Indian medicine	Waid
Baiha	An ornament worn on the left arm by women	
Bairi (+M)	Enemy	Wairi
Bairi	Hostility	Bair
Bairi;Dushman	Enemy	Bairi;Dushman
Baisak	April	Basakh
Baisau (+M) baisao	To settle	Wasao
Baisi	A panchayat; a council	Baithak
Baja (M)	A musical instrument	Baja; waja
Baja	To strike as a clock; time	Baja; wajia
Bajania (M)	A drummer	Dholi
Bajao (M)	To strike	Wajao
Bajar (M)	Bazar; market	Bazar
Bajar gathia	Undersized of juvenile	Githa
Baje (K)	Clock; watch; gong	Baje (time)
Baje	Some others; sometimes	Bajae
Bajha bajhi	To be entangled; to get into difficulties	Bhaj jana; phasna
Bajhao (M)	To seduce; to entangle	Bajhao. Nasao
Baji	To turn a summersault; to turn head	Bazi

	over heels	
Baji	Bet	Baji
Bajia	Sound	Wajia
Bajikor (K)	A juggler	Bazigar
Bajna (M)	To beat a drum	Wajna (dhol)
Bajnia	Drummer	Dohli
Bajra (M)	A grain	Bajra
Baju	An armlet worn above the elbow	Bajuband
Bak	The white paddy bird	Bag (bagla)
Bak-bak (K)	Headlessly	Bakbak
Bakao	To beguile; to mislead	Bakao (one whose loyalty can be bought)
Bakbakoak (M) Bakanra	To chatter; to gabble	Bakwas
Bakhac	Or else	Baadon
Bakhana bakhni	To prate; to jabber	Bakarwah; Bakwas
Bakhao	Babble	Bako
Bakhera	Wrangle; Disputation	Bakhera
Bakhor	Teeth of a comb	
Bakhra bakhri	To dispute angrily	Bakarwah
Baki	Balance; arrears	Baki
Baki;Kasar	Arrears	Bakaya
Bakjunu	The firefly	Jugnu
Bakoli	A poetical name for the white paddy	Bag; bagla

	bird	
Bakra (R)	Male lamb	Bakra
Bakra; Bakru	Male lamb	Bakra
Bakrara (R)	Shepherd	Aiali
Bakrarka (R)	Shepherd's wife	
Bakri (+R)	Female lamb	Bakri
Bakrisho; bakroro (R)	Lamb	Bkare
Baksa (+M)	An agricultural appliance; Cor.Eng. box	Baksa
Baksa (R)	Box; crate; wooden crate	Baksa
Bakshish (R)	Handout; tip	Bakhshish
Baksis (M)	A gratuity	Bakhshish
Baksis	Gratuity	Bakhshis
Bal (R)	Hair	Bal; wal
Bala-saka	Relations and friends of bride and bridegroom	Pb. sarbala is related to the word
Balae (M)	Difficulty; hardship; suffering	Bala
Balai	abundant; So very much as to cause surprise	Bala di
Balalo (R)	Covered with hair; hairy	
Balam (M)	Spear	Balam
Bale	Baby	Bal
Balgada	Sand carried down by flow of water	Bhal

Bali (R)	Loose woman; sow	Bali; bejan
Bali	Iron stone sand	Balo (rait; sand)
Bali Gur	Crystalized raw sugar	Gur
Balo (R)	Boar; male pig	Bhalu
Balok	Young; immature	Balak
Balti (+M)	A bucket	Balti
Bam	Shaft of a carriage	Bam
Baman (K) (+M) bamre	A Brahman	Bahman
Bambar (M)	Delirium; to talk nonsense	Bemar
Ban (+M)	Sorcery	Mand (mantra)
Ban (+M)	A flood	Banh (structure to stop water) and band seem to be derived from ban (flood).
Ban (K)	A dam; a band	Band
Ban (K)	To press upon; cruelty	Ban (arrow as well)
Ban	No; not	Ban bin
Banama	That is to say; namely	Banam
Banan	To spell	Bian
Banao	To make; to fashion	Banao
Banchao (M)	Salvation	Baca; bacao
Banchaoni (M)	Savior; protector	Bacaon wala
Band (M)	An	Band (dam)

	embankment	
Band	Embankment	Band
Banda pon	Money given by the guests at a wedding for the bride	Newndra pon; lag
Banda	To disgrace	Badnami
Bandh	An iron band round the nave of cart wheel to prevent it from splitting	Bandh
Bandha (M)	To mortgage; pawn or pledge	Bandha (Pb. slave)
Bandhao	To fix	Bandhao; banhna
Bandhe	To pledge; to pawn; to mortgage	Bandhe (utensils)
Bandhkok; Bandhoki; Bandki	To mortgage; Taking a mortgage &c.	Bandh
Bandho	Tie	Banho
Bandhon	A bond	Bandhon
Bandi	Young female	Bandi (female)
Bandkia	A person with a gun	Bandokia
Bandobos (K)	To make arrangements	Bandobast
Bandobos; bandobosto	To organize; to settle matters	Bondobast
Bandor	Monkey	Bandar
Banduk (M)	A gun	Banduk

Bani	Payment for services made in kind	Sapi
Bania (K)	Goldsmith	Pb. suniara; bania is money lender
Banij	To trade	Wanj (beopar)
Banij bepar	To trade	Wanj beopar
Banij	To trade	Wanj
Banij;Bepar	Trade	Banaj;Beopar
Banjh	Childless	Banjh
Banjha	Barren	Banjha
Banjha; bhanji	Childless (male and female)	Banjh
Banjhi	Childless female	Banjh
Bankhan; Bankhac	Or else; if not; otherwise	Balke
Banki	An anklet worn by women	Banki
Banria (M)	Merchant	Bania
Banu	Not to be	Bina
Banu; banuk	Not to be; not to exist	Bina
Banua	Unsocial; solitary; hermit like	Banua (from ban; jungle)
Banwas	To live in the forest	Banwas
Bao	Wind; breath; cholera	Wao; waba
Baosao; phaosao	Cox; wheedle	Phasao
Bap Dada;Purkha	Ancestors	Purkhe

Bap-purkha	Ancestors	Purkha
Bapa purkha	Ancestors	Purkhe
Bapa; bapu; bapo	Father	Bap; bapu
Baphao	To cook by steaming	Bhpao
Bapoti dhon	Paternal inheritance	Bap da dhan
Bapurce	Poor; miserable	Becare
Bar (K)	Outside; surface	Bahar
Bar (R)	Fence; barrier; hedge	Bar
Bar; babar (M)`	Two; twice	Bar (doji war)
Bar; barea	Tow	bar
Bara (M)	Senior; great grand-father	Wadha; bara
Bara	Expresses frequently; Continuance; habit	Wara
Bara	Habit	Wara (wartara)
Barabar	Continually	Barabar
Barabar; barabari (M)	Equal; Invariably	Barabar; barabari
Barac; badac	To know; to be cognizant	Wac; wacna
Barae	To know; to be cognizant of	Barae
Barai (M)	A blacksmith; one who melts iron	Barahi; lohar
Barakaiti (M)	Prosperity	Barkat
Baranda (K)	Verandah	Baranda

Barandi (M)	Any strong wine	Brandi
Barao (M)	To increase	Barao
Baras baris	Now and then; with intervals	Baras baris
Barbarao (M)	To speak meaningless word to oneself	Barbarao
Barchha (M)	Spear	Barcha
Barchi	A spear	Barchi (barshi)
Bardurce	A bat	Cancarik
Bare (M)	The banyan tree	Bor
Bare	Banyan	Bor
Bare-mosko (R)	Loud mouthed	Bara-monh
Bare-pelengo (R)	Well hung; displaying prominent male genitalia	
Barge	Garden	Bag
Barhao	To increae	Barhao; wadaho
Barhi (M)	Carpenter	Barhi; tarkhan
Barhiao	Growth	Barhiao; wadha
Barhon	Well grown	Bara; wadhia; wadho
Bari (M)	Flood	
Bari (R)	Important woman; female leader	Bari; wadhi
Bari	House	Mari (bari is window in Punjabi)

Baria	Bania	Bania
Bariat	Wedding procession	Barat; janj
Barilo (R)	Adult; grown up	Bala
Barimata; barimaatango (R)	Arrogance; haughtiness; ostentatious; vain; piggish	Bari-mat (wadh-mata)
Barisak (M)	Almost certainly	Baichak
Barjao;basti	populous	basti
Barket; Borket	Blessing	Barket
Barkhas	To dismiss	Barkhast
Barki (M)	A large size wrapper; a cloak	Burka
Barki	First wife	
Barmangao	To desire; to set one's heart on	War-mang (arranging marriage)
Barmon	Double minded	Doman; do-dalila; dalidar
Barnan;Biyan	Explain	Barnan;Biyan
Baro (R)	Big; great; large	Bara; wadha
Baro bakhan	To abuse	Bura bol
Baro bakhan; bisbakhan	To nag; to abuse; to call names; to vilify	Bara bakhan (wadhha backhand)
Baro-kar/kar-baro	Erect penis; erection	Baro (bra) kar (penis)
Baro-mui (R)	Loudmouth; overly opinionated	Bara-monhi

Barobar (K)	Always; incessantly	Barabar; brobor
Baromas	All the year	Baranmah
Baromasia; baramas	All the year round;	Baran-mah
Baron	To forbid; to taboo	Bandh
Bartan	A plate	Bartan (utensils)
Barti	Exceeding	Barti; wadhdi
Barud; baruj	Gunpowder	Barud
Barvalo (R)	Rich; wealthy man	Bara-vala (vala meaning possessor)
Bas khapao	To be past one's prime	
Bas	smell	bas
Bas;mahak	scent	bas;mahak
Basa (K)	A lodger; place	Basa
Basa	Residence	Wasa
Basao;Bandhao;Thahrao	Establish	Basana;Banhna;Thahrana
Basari (R)	Bass player	Bansir (derivation from bansary)
Base	Actually; really	Base
Basgadi	To settle permanently	Wasiba (was pena)
Basi (+M)	Stale; food prepared on the previous day	Basi; bahi
Basi mara	To allow a corpse to remain in the house	Basi mara

	overnight when it might have been disposed of before sunset	
Basia	Dirty	Busia; beha
Baskari; baslaria	Adept flute player	Bansria
Baskitia; Boskitia; Boskotia	Permanently settled	Basia; wasia
Basli (K)	A flute	Bansri
Basmati	A variety of rice	Basmati
Basti	A village	Basti; wasti
Basut	Property	Basat (like in bando bast)
Bat	Divide	Bant; wand
Bata	Exchange; discount	Bata (used in arithmetic for division)
Batai (K)	To explain; to make clear	Batai
Batar	Season; the proper time; state or condition	Watar
Bate; Raca	Courtyard of a house	Wahra
Batha (M)	Klin	Batha
Bathi (M)	Distillery	Bathi
Bati (M)	A lamp wick	Bati
Bati	A metal basin	Bati
Batil	Excess; surplus	Bahut; waphar
Batlao	To show; to point out	Batlao; daso

Batlao;Samjhao	Instruct	Samjhao
Bato (K)	To distribute	Bato
Batra	The pea	Matar
Batri	An ornament worn by women on the second toe	
Batu; Batua; batwi	A small bag	Batua; batwa
Bau (M)	Elder brother	Bhau; bhah
Baula (M)	Toothless	Bura
Baula	Insane	Bawara
Baura (+M)	Foolish	Bawara; buddho
Bayan; bean (+M) beana	To explain; a concocted story	Bayan
Bayar sandi	A cock kept for breeding purposes	Sand; saanh (male buffalo)
Ba'n ia (K)	Rather than	Bhane
Be-Bostor	Without clothing	
Be-ad	Without shelter; exposed	Be-than; be-ghar
Be-ae	Without measurement	Be-ae
Be-an	Without law	Be-aien
Be-as	Hopeless	Be-as
Be-batao	To disregard; to disobey	Be-behta
Be-bhagan	Unfortunate	Be-bhagan; abaghan
Be-bhorsa	No one to rely on	Be-bharosa

Be-dhob	Shapeless	Be-dhab
Be-dokhol	To evict	Be-dakhal
Be-hal	Destroyed; distressed	Be-hal
Be-hephajot	Uncared for	Be-hefazat
Be-hirla	To have no one to help	Be-hila
Be-hod; be-hudis	Dull; thick-headed	Be-hoda
Be-hok	Unjust; partial	Be-haq; na-haq
Be-hos; bi-hus (+M)	Unconscious	Be-hosh
Be-husnak	Ugly	Be-husnak; be-husan
Be-jaega	To evict one from his land or house	Be-jaga; be-dakhal
Be-juri	Not compatible	Be-juri; be-jur
Be-kam	Useless	Be-kam
Be-phaeda	Unprofitable	Be-phaeda
Be-rar	Out of tune; out of time	Be-sura
Be-rup	Change appearence	Be-rup; behrup
Be-sabab	Without reason	Be-sabab
Be-sagun	An evil omen	Be-sugan; bad-sugan
Be-sajon; be-sajonta	Unadorned; unfinished	Be-sajia; bena-sajan
Be-sak	Assuredly; without doubt	Be-shak
Be-tabe	Free; independenc	Be-tab (eager; impatient)

	e	
Be-thah; be-than	Bottomless	Be-thah
Be-thik	Incorrect	Be-thik; galat
Be-thir	Restless	Be-dhir; be-dhiraj
Beaj (+M)	Interest	Beaj; sud
Beakul	Restless	Beakul
Beamda	Without anyone to look to	Be-umeed
Bebak	All; the whole; without exception	Bebak (with no restraint)
Bebha	Simpleton	Bhola
Bebhar	To disgrace; to cause shame	Be-haya
Bebhorom	Disgrace	Behurmati
Becara	Poor; helpless; to be pitied	Becara
Bed	Vedas	Baid
Bedhao	To wrap around	Benhao; walao
Bedharak	Without any hesitation	Bedharak
Bedin	Heathen; atheist	Bedin
Bedisi (K)	A foreign land	Bides
Bedna	Pain; grief	Bedna; vedna
Bedoc	To make a slip; to mistake; to overlook	Be-wache
Bedoce		Dos

Bedon	Pain; grief	Bedon; vedon
Beg	A bag	Beg
Bega-ge (M)	Quickly; speedily	Beghai
Begar	Forced labour	Begar
Begar; beghor (+M)	Separate	Bghar
Begar; beth begar	Forced labor without pay	Begar; vegar
Begari; Bithi (+M)	Zemindars work without pay	Begari; vegari (Vegari; a profession included in artisans)
Behaj; bejae; behal	Astonshing; amazing	
Behde bhed	Accurately; in detail	
Behoea	Shameless; impertinent	Behoda
Behurmat; Bemurwat	To disgrace; to treat shamefully	Behurmat
Bei-man (K)	Falsely; untrustworthy	Bei-man
Beit (K)	Straight; right	Seit; Siedh
Bejae	Without	Bejae
Bejan	Without knowing; ignorantly	Bejan
Bejar	To be ill	Bezar
Bekar	Disguting	Bekar (of no use)
Beko	Brag	Bakna
Bekup	Stupid; foolish	Bewakof
Bela; bera	Time	Vela; wela

Belaiti (M)	Anything foreign	Walaiti
Belaur	A semi-precious stone	Belaur
Beldar	Caste of earth diggers	Beldar (bel means level)
Beli (R)	Supporting pole	Beli (Pb. beli; meaning friend may have this origin); thami
Belken	Young; infant; fresh	Bacpan
Belna	To roll dough into thin cakes	Belna; welna (a device or machine to process cotton; sugarcane etc
Belok	Separate; different	Begane
Bemal	Useless; spoilt	Be-mul
Beman; bemani	To show disrespect	Beman (from man)
Bemar; bemurad	Without relatives; without heirs	Bemar (ill)
Bemurwad	To disgrace; To outrage one's modesty	Be-murrawat
Benahak; benohok; benhak	Uselessly; causelessly; vainly; for no purpose	
Benao	To make; to prepare	Benao

Benc	A bench	Benc
Benden	Fasten	Banhana
Bengar	Brinjal	Baingan
Benjan binjin	Neither one thing nor the other	
Beohar	Behave	Vihar
Bepar (+M)	To trade	Bepar
Bepari (+M)	Trader; merchant	Bepari
Bepari	Trader	Beopari
Ber	Time; the sun; opportunity	Ver, vela
Beraji; beroj	Displeased; Unconsenting	Bezar
Beran	Colorless	Berang
Berbad	Destroyed	Barbad
Bero (R)	Rowboat; canoe; boat	Beri
Beros	Displeased; indisposed	Ros; rosna
Berot-duk	Any illness or disease the name of which is not known	Benan-dukh; anjana rug
Bersh (R)	Year	Baras; warha
Bertha	Unprofitable	Beartha
Besrom	Stubborn; self-willed	Besura
Besumar	Countless	Beshumar
Bet (+M)	A cane	Bet
Bet (K)	To sow	Bejna
Bet	Cane	Baint
Beta	Son	Beta

Beyakaran	Grammar	Beyakaran
Bgar	Mixed; impure; confused	Wagar; wigria
Bha	Well; good	Bha (like in bha jana)
Bhab	Friendship; love; sorrow	
Bhabi	To grieve; sorrow	Bhabi (sister-in-law)
Bhac bhac	To chatter; to gabble	Gup shup
Bhac bhacao	To chatter; to prate; to gabble	Bacar bacar
Bhacan bhucun	Restless	Bechen
Bhacan bhucun	Restless	Bechain
Bhado; bhador	The fifth solar month	Bhadon
Bhadob	Ugly	Bhada
Bhador	August	Bhadon
Bhag	portion	bhag
Bhagan; Bhagman	Fortunate	Bhagan
Bhagao	To divide; into shares or pieces	Bhagao (from bhag as share); wandao
Bhagao	To overcome; to make enemy run	Bhagao
Bhagat (M)	A witch finder	Bhagat
Bhagat	A vegetation	Bhagat (wild vegetation that grows in wheat crop)
Bhaggina (M)	Sister's son	Bhanja

Bhagiari; bhagidar	Share holder; partnerBhak	Bhagidar
Bhagin	Niece	Bhanji
Bhai	Brother	Bhai
Bhaiadi	Brothers; near relatives	Bradri
Bhaidi	Brothers	Bhai
Bhajan (M)	A religious song	Bhajan
Bhajra; bhajri	Talkative	
Bhak bokh	To speak nonsensically	Bak bak
Bhak		To bubble
Bhaka;Bhasa	Language	Bhaka;Bhasa
Bhakha	To brag; to boast	Bharak; bakhand
Bhakha;Boli	Dialect	Bhasha;Boli
Bhakhana bhakhani	Obscene talk	Bhakhan
Bhakti	pious	bhakti
Bhal bhal	Great; rich	Bhal bhal
Bhala	Well	Bhala
Bhalai	Benefit; profit; good	Bhalai
Bhalua	A swallow; a sand martin	Bhula
Bhan	Hemp	Phan
Bhan;Ganja	Hemp	Bhang;Ganja
Bhand	The vessel into which cows are milked	Bhanda (any vessel)
Bhand; bhond; bhandao	To defile ceremonially; to break a holy day	Bhand (to pollute by touching of lower caste; to make someone notorious)

Bhandar (M)	A granary; a store; treasury	Bhandar
Bhandar	store	bhandar
Bhandari (M) Bandhari	A house steward	
Bhang	Break	Bhang
Bhanga	To break; spoil; mar; undo; to break harmony	Bhang (rang mein bhang)
Bhangana;Bhatija	Nephew	Bhanja;Bhatija
Bhangao	To break; to destroy	Bhano
Bhangia muri	Half a bigha	Adh bigha
Bhangiabhat; bhanlabhat	To destroy	
Bhangot	Ruined; desolate and foesaken	Bhaj; bhanejia
Bhangrao (M)	To estrange	Bhano
Bhanj	To enquire into; to break	Bhanj
Bhanjao (M)	To change coins	Bhanao; bhan-banaho
Bhanka bakur		Cloth worn thin and at the point of tearing
Bhankur	The sound emitted by anything struck when drawn tight; a string &c.	Bhankur
Bhao (M)	Rate; price	Bhao; bha
Bhao	To prophesy;	Bhao

	to explain; to divine	
Bhaondao; Bhaorao	To disappear; to be lost	Bhondo
Bhaora	A boring instrument resembling a brace	
Bhaoria	One who peddles salt; tobacco; spices; etc and carries it in a basket on his head	Pheriwala
Bhaosao	To cox; to persuade	Phasao; bahkao
Bhap	Steam	Bhap
Bhaphao	To cook by steaming	Bhapao
Bhar (+M) bharom	Load; weight	Bhar
Bhar (M)	Full; whole	Bhar
Bhar bhar	To issue uninterpreted	Phar phar
Bhar juan	Prime of youth	Bhar jawan
Bhara (+M)	Rent; fare; to hire; to rent	Bhara
Bhara bhuru	Easily powdered; loose; soft	Bhubura
Bhara;Mahsul	Freight	Bhara;Masul
Bharabhat	To destroy; to waste	Barbad
Bharao	Fill	Bharo

Bhari	Heavy	Bhari
Bharia	A stick on which anything to be carried is placed ; carried over one shoulder	
Bharkhar	In full swing	Bharpur
Bharna	The name given to the woof by weavers	
Bharosa (M)	Expectation; hope	Bharosa
Bharosa;Biswas	Faith	Bharosa;Biswas
Bharsak	Full force or ability	
Bharti (+M)	To enlist or recruited	Bharti
Bhas	Knowledge; ability	
Bhasakar	Ugly; unshapely	Badchakal
Bhasam	Ashes	Bhasam
Bhasao	To be carried away by water	Bhahao
Bhasi	Nature; custom; habit; disposition	
Bhaskao	To burst out; to burst only and contents shattered	Phatna

Bhat	A beggar	Bhat; faqir
Bhata	Furnace	Bhata
Bhatao	To fill up; to level up	Bharna
Bhathi	A boiler; a copper	Bhathi (small furnace to heat up; roast or melting)
Bhati (M)	Grog shop	Bhati
Bhati	The kernel of certain fruits when half ripe	Bhutta
Bhaya	Brother	Bhaya
Bheao	To recognize; to know	Bojho
Bhed (+M)	Interpretation; meaning; inner meaning; reason	Bhed (secrete)
Bheda	A ram	Bhedo
Bheja; bhejao	Sent	Bheja; ghalia
Bhejer Bhejer	To jabber; to chatter	Bhecar bhecar
Bhek	Heavily	Bhar; buhat
Bhenjan	To mix; to mingle	
Bhenta	A word or a phrase with double meaning	Bait; baint
Bhes	Form or appearence	Bhes
Bhesa bhisi	To copy eachother	

Bhesao	To mimic; to mock	
Bhet	A visit of condolences especially by women	Mukan (probably from mukan)
Bhetuak	An ornamental band for the hair	
Bhidata	Hindu deity	Data
Bhidi	A sheep	Bhid
Bhidia; Bhiduk	Spy	Bhidia; jasos
Bhijau	To soak in	Bhijia
Bhikari	A beggar	Bhikari
Bhikhari	Beggar	Bhikhari
Bhili gur	A large lump of raw sugar	Bhili gur; paisi gur
Bhili	The distance between two furrows	Word paili may have been derived from it. Otherwise called siarh in Punjabi
Bhilki	Afraid	Bhiliki (like Bhigi billi)
Bhim		
Bhina; bhina bhini;	To separate; to disagree; to divide	Bhin bhin. (may be bhirna)
Bhind	A bale; a faggot; a mass; a lump	Pand; bhari
Bhinda	A lump; applied specifically to the mass of	Pand

	iron taken from the smelting furnace.	
Bhingrau	To lead astray; to cause to err	Wigaru
Bhir	Crowd	Bhir
Bhirau	To press close	Bhirau (of bodies; like in bhir)
Bhirkau	To be frightened	Bharkao (is the closet but that mean to flare up)
Bhirobhoro	To crack; as an earthen vessle	Bhor; bhur jana
Bhisor	A mistake; an error	Besor; besur
Bhitar	Inside	Bhitar
Bhitar; bhitri	Inside	Bhitar
Bhitir	Within	Bhitar
Bhoco	Stupid; foolish	Ghocho; bhudo
Bhoda	Fat; Corpulent; dull headed	Bhoda
Bhodran	Worthy; respectable	Pardhan
Bhoe	Fear	Bhoe
Bhog	To enjoy; To feel pleasure; middle	Bhog
Bhogot	A jogi	Bhagat
Bhoj	Feast	Bhoj
Bhok	To bark	Bhonk

Bhonda	Ceremoniously unclean	Bhonda
Bhor; bhorao	Full; whole; to fill	Bharia; bharna
Bhori	One tola or the weight of one rupee	Bhori
Bhorma; bhormi	Secretly; without display; privately	Bhora (bhore paina)
Bhorna	Secretely; without display; privily	Bhorna (bhore paina)
Bhorok	Apprehensive of danger	Bhirak
Bhorom-sorom (M)	Shyness	Bhorom sorom
Bhorosa	Hope; dependence; trust	Bhorosa
Bhorosa	Trust	Bharosa
Bhorsa	Confidence	Bharosa
Bhorsak;bharsak	With all one's strength	
Bhosa	To pierce through; to stab	Ghosa (ghosana; ghopana)
Bhosam; puta	The first stomach	Puta
Bhosando	Slovenly; dirty; dusty	Bhusia; busia
Bhota	To besmear oneself with ashes like jogis	Bhota (bhobhot laona)

Bhoyon	Fear; frightful; fearful	Bhoya (struck by bhoh)
Bhua	Idle; false	Bhua (Pb. undeservedly angry)
Bhucamp;Bhuical	Earthquake	Bhuchal
Bhucampa	An earthquake	Bhuncal
Bhugol	Geography	Bhugol
Bhujantar	Wise; clever; sharp	Bhujantar
Bhuk duk	Distress; sorrow	Dukh
Bhuktan	To pay in full	Bhugtn
Bhul cuk	omission	bhul chuk
Bhul	Forget	Bhul
Bhul; bhul cuk	Mistake; error	Bhul
Bhulao	To forget; to cause to forget; to decieve	Bhulao
Bhulkau	To gush out; to flow out; to spring as water	Bhurkna
Bhumbri	Small pimple	Bhumbri
Bhumi	Land	Bhumi; zamin
Bhungar	A piece of wood	Budgar (bugdar; a piece of round wood lifted to show strength)
Bhurbhuri	To rain; sparks	
Bhuri	To untwist; to	Bhuri (a blanket

	uncoil; to take off cloths that are fastened around the waist	worn by mystics)
Bhurke	To fill in ; to dip a vessel in water to fill it	Bharna; Purna
Bhurti	To fill up; whole	Purti
Bhus; Bhusun	Suddenly	Bhus
Bhusa	Chaff	Bhusa (turi)
Bhusri	Applied to girls when scolding	Bhusri
Bhut (+M) (+K)	A demon; a ghost	Bhut
Bhut	Demon	Bhut
Bhut;Jin	Ghost	Bhut;Jin
Bhutaha	A haunted place; occupied by bhuts	
Bhutan	Angry	
Bhutel; bhuter	Like a demon	Bhuter
Bhuter	To excess; over much	Bhuter
Bhuti (M)	A day labor	Pb. To have someone work promising to compensate in someway; buta; also means deceiving
Bhutka	Small;	Chutka

	Darwish	
Bi (R)	Without; this is prefixed to many descriptive adjective; past participle adjectives and adverbs to form their opposite	Bi
Bi-Zorako; bi-zoralo(R)	Helpless; ineffective; without power	Be-zor
Bi-darako	Brave; fearless	Be-darako; nadar
Bi-darano	Unafraid	Be-dar
Bi-devlesko (R)	Atheist	Be-dev-lesko (his) (dev di hasti nun na mannan wala)
Bi-dikhlo (R)	Imaginary; invisible	Be-dikhia; an-ditha
Bi-doshako; bi-doshwalo (R)	Innocent; without blame	Be-dosh; bedos
Bi-dukhado (R)	Unhurt; uninjured	Be-dukh; bedukh
Bi-gindo (R)	Uncounted	Be-ginia; anginia
Bi-ginimasko (R)	Innumerable	Be-ginti; beshumar
Bi-grizhako (R)	Carefree; without responsibilities	Be-garz; la-garz

Bi-kardo (R)	Unfinished; undone	Be-kardo; be-keta
Bi-manglo (R)	Not requested; unasked	Be-mangia
Bi-manushwalo (R)	Inhuman	Be-munash-wala
Bi-masalo (R)	Vegetarian	Be-masala (masala seems to related to â€˜mas’)
Bi-merimasko (R)	Eternal; undying	Be-marna
Bi-pako (R)	Immature; unripe	Be-paka
Bi-phanglo (R)	Loose; released; untangled; unbound	Be-phasia
Bi-pushlo (R)	Without asking; without permission; uninvited	Be-pucho
Bi-suto (R)	Sleepless	Be-suta
Bi-tango (R)	Loose; not tight	Be-tangia
Bi-wuzho (R)	Unclean; Impure	Be-wuzu
Bi-yakhako (R)	One-eyed	Be-wekhana; kana
Bia (K)	To marry	Viah
Biar (K)	A wall	Dewar
Bibad	Enmity; ill will	Anad
Bibhorom	To disgrace; to outrage one’s	Bipharna

	modesty	
Bibi (R)	Aunt; term of respect for any elderly woman; matriarch	Bibi (Pb. used for mother also)
Bibi	Anything that frightens or hurts	
Bibilau	Soft as a fruit	Pilpila
Bibiyo (R)	Auntie	
Bichar (+M)	To judge; to consider	Wichar
Bichar (M)	To judge; to conclude	Wichar (to think)
Bichar	Decide	Bichar
Bichia	A ring worn on the second toe by women	
Bichiri (M)	To divide into thin pieces	Biciri (bajri)
Bichnan; bichnao	To recognize; to discern	Pichan
Bichri	To separate; to split	Bichri
Bid (M)	To plant in the ground	Bijna
Bida (+M)	To bid farewell	Bida; wida
Bida (R)	Trouble; difficulty	Weda; waeda
Bidal	Generation; time	
Bidan	To test; to tempt; to	Widwan

	prove	
Bides	Foreign	Bides;Pardes
Bidesi;Pardesi	Foreigner	Bidesi;Pardesi
Bidesia	Foreigner	Bidesia
Bidha; Bidhi	Custom; usage; mode	Bandh
Bidhua; Bidhwa	Born out of wedlock	Harami
Bidia; bidya	Knowledge	Widia
Bidia;bed bidia	Hinderance; adverse influence of supernatural order	
Bidot	To cause suffering or shame	Bidot (to break religious dictate)
Bidraha	Strayed; lost	Bidraha
Bidya	Learning	Vidya
Biecit (K)	Foolish; dumb; disabled	Be-dmag
Bigha	A measurement of land; from Â½ to ¼ of an acre	Bigha
Bigiria	Forced labor	Bigari; wegari
Bigra bigri	To astray; to pervert	Bigra; bigri
Bih (K)	Poison	Weh; zahar
Biha	Marriage	Wiha
Bihar	To explain	Wihar
Bijar	Sorrowful; grievous	Bezar
Bijau	To be	Bijau; bhijia

	saturated	
Bijir bijir	To be turned into small pieces	Pichir pichir
Bijli	Lightening	Bijli
Bikan	To be sold	Wikan
Bikau	To be sold or disposed	Bikau
Bikau	sold for a price	bikau
Bikhar	Enmity; not on speaking terms	Wigar
Bikol; bikoli	Restless	Bikal; wiakal
Bil (M)	To spread	Phel
Bil	A bill; an account	Bil
Bilan; biland; bilat	A wide expanse; a plain	Maidan
Bilat	To lend money on interest	Biaj
Bilati	Things of England	Wilaiti
Bilbilau; chilbilau	To cry in pain	Bilbilau
Bilka (M)	To feel pity	Bilka; wilka
Bin kaneur	The slough of a snake	Kunj; skunj
Bin	A snake	Bin (snake charmer's music instrument)
Bin; bina	Without	Bin; bina
Bind	A pin of wood used instead of a nail	Bind

Binda (+M)	A sheaf; a bundle	Binda. Bhari; (bir is the straw rope to tie the bundle of grain or rice. Bir may be derived from binda.
Bindi	Spider	Bindi
Bindu (M)	Upper-ear ring	Bunde
Bing (M)	Snake	Bin in Santhali; Pb. the musical instrument to charm the snakes
Binhak; binhakte	Falsely; without cause	Binhak; nahak
Binti (M) Binti	To discuss; to peach; relate; exhort; teaching (M) beseech	Binti (to request; to beg)
Bipod;Duk	Trouble	Bipat;Dukh
Bir (M)	Jungle	Bir; bar
Bir disom	The forest country	Bir des
Biragi (M)	Alone; lonely	Biragi; biragin
Biran; birana	Foreign; country at distance	Biron; wiran
Birbanta	A giant; a minghty man of valor	
Birbao	Hurricane; cyclone	
Birhau	To begin to	Birahu

	grow	
Birhor	A Dravidian jungle tribe	
Biri	A chain put on prisnors' ankle	Biri
Birin birid	Weeping and sobbing	Wain
Birin	Bearing; a letter without stamp	Birang
Birkau	Frightened	Birik jana
Birki	Frightened	Birki (bidki)
Birla	some	birla
Birodhi	Angry; at variance	Wirodhi
Birot	Enmity	Wirodh
Birudh (M)	Against	Wirudh
Bis	Twenty	Bih
Bis; Bisi (+M)	Poison	Bis; wis
Bisal	Poisoned arrow	Bisal
Bisbakhan	To abuse; to say all the bad things against other	
Bisbiswas; biswas (M)	Certainly; without doubt	Wachwach
Bish (R)	Twenty	Bis; wih
Bishwar (R)	Twenty times	Bis bar; wih war
Bisi	To increase; more	Bisi
Bisor	Mistake	Bisur
Bisti (K)	Water carrier	Bihichti; machki
Bistor	Many; much	Be-chumar

Bit	To plant	Bijna
Bita	A span; to measure by spanning	Bita; minia
Bitan	To pass time or life	Bitan
Bitar (M)	Inside	Bhitar
Bithi; Bithiahi	Forced labor	
Biti	Daughter	Beti
Biti; Kuri	Daughter	Beti;Kuri
Blang	A goat	Bakri
Bod; Kharap	Bad	Bad; Kharab
Bod;Dustu	Evil	Bad;Dusht
Bodla; bodol	To exchange	Badla
Bodmas	A rascal	Badmach
Bodnam	With a bad name; notorious	Badnam
Bodo	Stupid	Bodho
Bodoce	To squeeze; wring out	Nocore
Bodre	Old	Bodre
Boe	To stammer	Thathlana
Boela	Tall	
Bohao	To be floated away	Bohao
Bohi	Flowing	Rurhi
Bohni (M)	To make the first sale of the day for cash	Bohni
Bohoe	To swill cloths in water; wash	Bhagoi
Bojao (M)	To understand;	Bojao

	to perceive	
Bojao	To load; to load a gun	
Bojh; bojha	Burden	Bojh; bojha (pocket)
Bokao	To chatter; to jabber	Bokao (bak bak)
Bokh; bokhalo; bokhawol (R)	Hunger; hungry	Bokh; bokha
Bokobhand	To disgrace	Bokhand
Boksa	A warlock who is known for magic	
Bol	Strength; might	Bal
Bolahat; Phukar	Call	Bulana;Pukar
Bolahat; bolhat	To call; warrant	
Bole	Saying	Bole
Boli; buli	Language	Boli
Bolo (+M)	To enter	Pb. boha and barohan are derived from bolo
Bolom (M)	A spear	Bolo; bhala
Bonat	Agreement; peace; harmony	Bana ke
Bond	To close	Bond
Bondo	Foolish; stupid	Bondo (bhondo)
Bonga Kuri		Bonga kuri
Bonga kora	A demon which takes the form of man or	Bonga munda

	woman	
Bonga	A demon; Santhalis's devta	Bonga (foolish; stupid)
Bonkor	Tax for the forest products	
Bonolo (M)	Entrance; gate	Boha
Bonorsa (M)	Hope; expectation	Bharosa
Bor	Thick straw rope used principally to bind rice bundles	Bir
Bor; botor	Fear; dread	
Bora (M)	Blunt; toothless	Bora
Bora	Bag	Bora
Borkao	To frighten	Birkao
Borket	prosperity	barkat
Borket; Barket	Blessing	Barkat
Borkhas	Dismiss	Barkhast
Boro (M)	To frighten; to be frightened; fear; fright	Boh
Borop	Ice	Barf
Borti	To enlist	Bharti
Bortia (M)	Bridegroom's party	Barat
Bos	Children; generation	Posh
Boskot; boskoti; boskotia	Dwelling place; to	Waskot (was-kot)

	inhabit	
Bosri	A prostitute	Bosri (used as abuse)
Bosta	A sack; a bag	Bosta; basta
Bosti	Populous; large	Basti; wasti
Bosto	To destroy; to ruin	Bhos (like in zamin-bos)
Bostor	Cloth	Vastar
Botolo (M)	Bottle	Botal
Bud (M)	Wednesday	Budh
Bud; budhi	Wisdom	Bud; budhi
Buda	Stock; root	Muda
Budakil	Understanding	
Budan	Wise	Wadwan
Budhi ayo	Grandmother	Dadi
Budhi	sense	budhi
Budhia	Mother	Bhuri
Bufari/bukfari (R)	Wallet; pocketbook	Butwa
Bugli	A small bag; a purse	Bugli
Buhel	Flow	Bahna
Buhni (M) Bohni	First sale of the day	Bohni
Buj bujhau	To distinguish between wrong and right	Bujh bujhao
Buj;Bujhao	Understand	Bujhna
Bujha bujhi	To consult each other	Bujha buji
Bujhao	Comprehend	Bujheya
Bujhao;Samjhao	Convince	Samjhao;Bujhao
Buklo (R)	Wooden	Buka

	container for water	
Bulahat	Summons; calling	Bulahat
Bulau	To mislead	Bhulao
Bule (R)	Indulge in sexual intercourse	Pb. bule lutna; balad may be from this origin
Bunayadi	Aboriginal	Kabayali
Bund	Drop	Bund
Bundi; bindi	To put a red mark on forehead	Bindi
Bunduk	Gun	Bunduk
Bunia	Foundation	Buniad
Buniad	Origin; foundation	Buniad
Buniadi	First original	Buniadi
Bur (M)	To make a hole	Bur
Bura (M)	To fill a vessel by dipping into water	Burna
Burha;Burhi	Aged	Burha Burhi
Burha;budi	old	burha;burhi
Burj; burunj	A tower	Burj
Burubera (M)	Flat and level	Brubur
Buruj	Tower	Burj
Burus	Brush	Burus
Busku	To exasperate	Buskna
But (R)	Many; much; a lot	Buhat; bahon
Buta (M)	The stem	Buta
Buta	The origin of the tree	Buta (a tree as well)

Buter (R)	More	Bahtera
Butra (R)	Short in stature	Buna
Butri	Female short	Buni
Butwar (R)	Often; many times	Buhar-war; bahonwar
Buya	The female organ	
Byna (K)	To be informed; to hear	Bian
	C	
Cab (M)	To yawn	Pb. To grind under teeth
Caba (M)	To finish; end; an action to complete something	Chaba lena
Caba	To finish; to complete; to die; all; the whole	Pora
Cabao	To swallow; to devour	Cabao
Cablan	To bite; to fix; to teeth into	Cabna
Cabuk	A horse's whip	Cabuk
Cacak	Tattered	Cak; patia
Cada cadi	Divorce	Cada cadi; talaq
Cader; cadra	A cotton cloth	Cader; cadra
Cadra (M)	Cloth sheet	Cadar; cadra
Caecor	A gypsy tribe	Caecor

	known for stealing	
Caego	Talkative; clapper tongued	Cahga
Cagat	To detach	Cagat (frame of cot)
Cahak mahak	To be eager; intent	Cahak mahak
Cahao	To wish	Cahao
Cahe	Perhaps; whether; or	Cahe
Caher	Shadow; reflected image; appearance	Capa
Cahi; cahia	Needful; wanted	Cahi; cahia
Cak (M)	A wheel	Chak
Cak bandhi	A cog put before the wheel to prevent it moving	Cak bandhi
Cak	A wheel	Cak
Cakap cakap	Noise while eating	Cakap Cakap
Cakar	Circle; to make a horse run in a round for training	Cakar
Cakha	To taste	Cakha
Caki	A flat cake cut into thin pieces	Caki (like of soap)

Cakla coklo	Dodging through fear or shame	Cakla
Cakmak (M)	To shine	Chamak
Cakmak	Shining	Cakmak; jagmag
Cakor	A servant for non-agricultural services	Cakar
Cakri ghum	Dizzy; confused	Cakri ghum; cakr aona
Cakri	Service	Cakri
Caktatc	How	Keunkar
Caku	A knife with handle	Caku
Cal	Conduct; behavior	Cal; cala
Cala calak	To move; to pass away	Cala
Calak	Go	Chalo
Calak;Hilau	Move	Chal;Hill
Calaki	Deception	Chalaki
Calan	Consignment	Chalan
Calao (M)	To set in motion; to drive; to manage	Chalao
Calao	Administer	Chalana
Calcal	Movement	Chalna;Chaal
Calcolon	Character	Calcolon
Calcul	To begin to move	Calcul
Cali	Custom; usage	Cali
Camac	A spoon	Camac
Camaota; campata	A strap of	Camota (used by

	hide	bhands in making jokes)
Camar	A caste or profession dealing with hides	Camar
Camkao; camkan	To flash	Camkao; camkan
Campa	A small shrub with yellow or red flowers	Campa
Camta		Campta
Camuk	A whip	Cabuk
Cand	Necessary; urgent; quickly; firmly	Cand (a few)
Canda (M)	Subscription; rent; contribution	Chanda
Canda	A contribution	Canda
Candal	Wicked; licentious	Candal
Candal;Luca	Vicious	Chandal;Lucha
Candan (M)	Sandal tree	Chandan
Candan	Sandal wood	Candan
Candi (M)	Silver	Chandi
Candi	Forehead	Candi
Candoro; Candro	Flirting; wanton	Candra
Candu (M)	Moon	Chan; chand
Canke	Waiting in for a prey; fierce; furious	Canke
Caora	Having the	Jura

	long hair in the tail more or less white	
Cape; cupe	Secretly; quietly	Cupe
Capit	Secrete	Chupia
Capra	Broken	Chowra
Capu	To examine; to explore	Catao; Jacu
Car	Four	Char
Cara	Fodder	Chara
Carcari	Irritated; a scourge	Carcari
Carha	More; rise	Carha
Carhao	Irritate	Chirao
Carhi	To increase; gone up	Carhi
Cariau	To incite; to instigate	Cariau
Cario kor	All around	Car cupher
Carkha (M)	Spinning wheel	Carkha
Carkhi	A machine used to separate the seeds from cotton	Wailna
Carot	Pasture for the cattle	Carot (caragah in Urdu)
Carwahi	Compensation of a shepherd	Charwai; carai
Cat	Immediately; quickly	Jhat
Catai	A panchayat; a meeting	Catai (a mat)

Catak cutuk	To lick the lips	
Catak mente;	Immediately; quickly	Cutki maran wich
Catan	A massive stone	Catan
Catna	Living on others	
Catni	Female for Catna	
Catpat	Immediately	Jatpat
Catpatao; chatpatao	Quickly	Jhat nal
Catti	Where travelers pass night	Saran
Catue (M)	Earthen pot; a pitcher	Cati
Catur	Clever; shrewd; scheming	Catur
Caucal	A babbler	Cancal
Cauka	A measure of the earthwork	Cauka (culah cauka; a square where food is cooked)
Caukidar	Watchman	Chaukidar
Cauli (M)	Rice	Caul
Caupohor	All four times of the day	Caupahar
Cece	Squeal of birds	Cechana
Cechor; chechor; cecor	Mischievous; tricky	Chechora
Cedao	To let go free	Cedao
Cedke	Wherefore	Kedre
Cehao	To warn; to	Jetao

	be cautious	
Cehra	Face	Cehra
Cela	A disciple	Cela
Cenda kura	A 15 year old boy	Nwan munda
Centa (M)	Envy; jealousy; cleverness	Centa
Cepa	A piece of turf	Cepa
Cepat	To be master of; proficient	
Cepe; cepra	Flat	Cepe
Ceped (M)	To lick; to suck	Catna
Cepo; ceped (M)	Flat	Cepta
Cere	Sparrow	Ceri
Cetak	To slap	Cat; canta
Cetan	Over; above; on	Cetan
Cetao (M)	To advise; to bring to senses	Cetao
Cetao	Warn	Chetao
Cetaona	Warning	Cetaona
Cete (M)	Cunning; clever; deceitful	Pb. remember
Cete	To learn; to teach	Cete
Cethra	A rag; old worn out cloths	Cethra
Cethrece	A rag	Cethra
Cha (+M)	Tea	Cha
Chaba	To print	Chapa

Chabha	A small earthen pot	Chabha (A flat basket for bread)
Chabi	Key	Chabi
Chaches (R)	Fairly; really; truly	Saci; caj
Chad	Allowable; not forbidden; free	Chad; chut
Chae	Quickly	Cheti
Chaela (M)	Ornamental; showy; love of pleasure; one addicted to songs and dances;	Chaela; chail
Chaeman (M)	To disappear; to vanish; as by magic	Chaenmaen
Chai (R)	Tea	Cai; ca
Chaila (M)	Chips of wood	Picar
Chailke	A chip of wood	Chilat
Chainiko (R)	Teapot	Cainak
Chakacur	To shatter to pieces	Cakcur; ciknacur
Chakao	To be separated by filtering	Chanana
Chakha (M)	To taste	Cakha
Chakmak	Flint	Chakmak
Chal chal	Hurriedly; quickly	Calacal
Chal challan (M)	Behavior	Cal calan
Chal	Bark;	Chal; chilar

Chala (M)	A sieve	Shanani
Chala	Panniers	Chala
Chala Badla	A pack bullock	Chala Bald
Chalak (M)	Artful; deceitful	Calak
Chalak chandori	A lascivious woman	Chalak chandori (candri)
Chalan (M)	To take away to jail	Calan
Chalchalao	To cut through the water	Chalchalao
Chale	Scum rising to the surface of any liquid	Chal
Chalkao	To pare; to skim	Chalkao
Cham cham	Sound produced by toe rings when the wearer walks	Cham cham
Chama (M)	To forgive	Chama
Chamak damak	To show off	Chamak (Pb; Chamak also means a thin tree branch)
Chamak	Tinkling	Chamak
Chambal (R)	Chew; munch; ruminate	Caban; cabna
Chamda	Temporary tent to accommodate guests	Chamiana

Chamta (M)	A leather strap to bind the yoke with the plough haft	Camata
Chan	To strain out	Chan (from chanana)
Chanda (M)	Contribution	Canda
Chaora	Immature; not full grown	Chora
Chap; chapa		To print
Chapar dake	Saline water	Khara pani
Chapkao (M) Chapao	To hide	Chapkao (chapao)
Chaplau	To overflow	Chalkao
Chapri (+M)	A hut; a roof	Chapri
Char (R)	Grass	PB. carna; as shepherding; derived from this
Char	Suddenly; at once	Jhat
Chara (M)	Food for animal	Cara
Chara-chenri	A sparrow	Cira-ciri
Charao	To grow; to increase	Carao
Charra	Gun shot	Charra
Chat	To separate; to pare	Chat (chant)
Chat	Roof	Chat
Chat-patia (M)	Restless	Jhat-patia
Chat; chat chat; chat marte	Suddenly; quickly	Jhat; jhat pat; jhat karke
Chatak	A measure; two ounces	Chatank

Chatao (M)	To lick	Catao
Chatar	An umbrella	Chatri
Chati phatao	To burst the heart; to rend the heart	Chati phatao
Chati	Breast	Chati
Chatka; Chatka duar	Door from the courtyard to the street	Phatak
Chatna; chatni	Top; highest; pinnacle	Coti
Chatpat	Quickly	Jhatpat
Chatur (M)	Cunning; to decieve	Catar
Chauktha	Frame	Chaukath
Chauni	Encampment; resting place during a journey; a tent; a roof	Chauni (military headquarters)
Chauni;Tambu	Tent	Chanani;Tambu
Chazhma (R)	Water fountain	Cachma
Che (R)	What; which	Che (Persian); keh
Cheala juan	A well grown healthy youth	Chela juan
Chechor; Cechor; cecor	Tricky; mischievous	Chechora
Chedua; chedui	Separated couple	Chedua; cheduwi; chuttar
Chek	Nipping	Chek (Pb. hole)
Chekunalao; chekunil (R)	Fatty; greasy	Ceknai
Chela (M)	A disciple	Cela
Chepo (R)	Cork; bottle stopper	Capni

Cherea (M)	A shepherd or goat herd	Chero
Cherko (R)	Hoop; rim	Cak; cakar; carkha
Chi (M)	What?	Keh
Chi chi	Shame	Chi chi
Chi tho	To feel disgusted	Chi tho
Chij;Jinis	Thing	Cheej;Jins
Chikako (R)	Adobe; made of clay mud	Chikako (chak is used by potter to mold wet clay into earthen vessles)
Chikin (M)	A female ghost	Curail
Chinar	A harlot; a prostitute	Chinal
Chingar (R)	Altercation; brawl; fight	Cagra; jhagra
Chingarash; chingril (R)	Argumentative male person; squabble	Jhagralo; jhageil
Chink (R)	Sneeze	Chink; chik
Chirao (M)	To excite anger	Cirao
Chirha chirhi	Increasing; violently	Cira; ciri
Chiri biri	Into small pieces	Ciri biri
Chit	Stained; spotted	Chit
Chita	To accuse falsely	Chitan paona (derivation chat)
Chitau	To spread	Chitau

	sheaves on the threshing flor for the grain to be trodden out by cattle	
Chitia bitia	To scatter	Chitia bitia
Chitkau	To sprinkle	Chirkau
Chobanka (R)	Shepherd's wife	Cobanika
Chobano (R)	Shepherded	Coban
Chol; chole; chol kopot	Fraud; artificial; deception	Chawal
Chond kora; kuri	A boy from 12 to 14; a girl from 8 to 10	Chond (braided hair) Pehle chondian nal handaya ee; Waris Shah)
Chor (R)	Embezzler; grafter; robber; thief	Cor
Chorecherao	To irritate; to sting; to rile	Chorecherao
Chorkot	Waste; to spend	Chorkot
Chorni (R)	Female thief	Corni
Chot	Time	Jhat
Chuc	Needle	Sui
Chuchi	Female breast; nipples	Cuci
Chuchiwali (R)	Big breasted	Cuciwali
Chuchkar	To address kindly	Chuchkar
Chuchundar (M)	A musk rat	Chuchundar

Chudato (R)	Abnormal; bizarre; weird	Chudai
Chugnil (R)	Lash; whip	Chainta (derivation)
Chumba (M)	Any foreign substance which has entered the eye	Chumba
Chumi (R)	Kiss	Cumi
Chumidemos (R)	Kissing	Cumna
Chumidyol (R)	Kissed	Cumia
Chundi	A girl	Chuhri
Chunnri (R)	She braids/weaves braids	Cunri (cloth covering head seems related)
Churi	Knife	Chhuri
Churo (R)	Sieve; strainer	Chanani
Chuta (+M) chutao	Free	Chuta
Chuta (M)	Tuft of the hair on the crown of the head	Chuta
Chuta	Divorce	Chhuta
Chutan	To escape; to be let loose	Chutan
Chuti (+M)	Leave	Chuti
Chutki	Second wife	
Cia (M)	Why	Keon
Cia	To spy; to search for	
Cigari	To mock	Cagh
Cigi	To be impaled through the	Ciki

	fundament	
Cij (+M) Chij	Thing in general; agricultural product	Ciz
Cikan	Smooth	Cikna
Cilim	The bowl of the huka in which the fire and tobacco are placed	Cilim
Cimta (M)	Pincer	Cimta
Cinda;Cando	Moon	Chand
Cindal	A little here and a little there	Calu
Cini (M)	Sugar	Cini
Cinta	Pincers	Cimta
Cinte	Thought	Chint
Cir	A flag	Cir (turban)
Cira; ciro	To tear; split	Cira
Cirha cirhi	Violently	Cirah
Cirhau		To scoff at; deride; to provoke
Citar-kabar (M)	Spotted	Cit-kabra
Citerbiter (M)	Scattered	Titerbiter
Citha	A note; a written order	Citha
Cithi (+M)	A letter	Cithi
Citri	The grey partridge	Titar
Ciulao (M)	Ever; at any time	Calu
Ciunti	An ant	Ciunti; Keri
Coak	To break; to	Coak

	snap	
Cobuce	To prick	Cobuh; cobuhna
Cocraha	Rough	Cerah
Codak; Codao; Chondao; Cotak	To detach	Cadna; Cilna
Coe	Part of female private member	Choan
Coelo; Cuila	Sharp; pointed	Cula
Cok	Village square	Cok
Coko	The female organ	Cut
Colon; Colonti	Custom; use; current	Calan
Concol	Frickle; restless; excited	Cocol (cancal)
Cond	Sample; selection	Cond
Condho	An abuse; scoundral	Codho (may be related to chut or codna)
Copoce	To suck (as an orange)	Copana
Corke coroke	To move by leaps like frog	Carape
Cot	Above; high	Coti
Cu; co (M)	To kiss	Cumna
Cubao	Bite	Chabana
Cucu; cucke	The female organ	Cut
Cudi	To go backward; as	Cudi

	if ashamed	
Cugli capati	Backbiting	Cugli
Cugli	Backbite	Chugli
Cuglia	Backbiter	Cuglia
Cui	A well	Khui; khuh
Cuk (+M)	An error	Cuk (as in bhul cuk)
Cuk;Bhul	Mistake	Bhul
Cuka (M)	A small earthen pot	Kuja
Cukao	To finish	Cukao
Culha (+M)	Fire place	Culha
Culha	Fireplace	Chulha
Culti	Customary; usual	Calti
Cuman (M)	Ceremony of kissing before marriage	Cuman
Cumdine	An abusive woman	
Cun	Lime	Chuna
Cuna (M)	Lime	Cuna
Cunci	Nipple	Chuchi
Cunda; cundi	The youngest of the family	Cunda; cundi
Cuni	Small	Cuni
Cunka	A pinch given by the seller to buyer above purchased thing	Cunga
Curi (+M) curia	A bracelet; a bangle	Curi
Curi	Bangle	Churi
Curti	To increase;	Carti

	to develop	
Cuti (M)	The point at top of everything	Cuti
Cutia (+M) cautu	A mouse	Cuha
Cutki	To snap the fingers	Cutki
Cuwa	To distil	Cuna
	D	
Da (K)	By; with; through	Us da
Da (M)	Give me	De
Da-catu (M)	Water pot	Cati (pani)
Da-rape-jot	To make a lame excuse	Da-dapa; jot-da (da meaning clever move)
Dab (M)	Hastily; quickly; suddenly	Daba ke
Dab (R)	Bang; blow; jab; knock; punch	Dab
Dab	An accident; mishap	Dab
Dab-tari (K)	A handle of a knife	Daftri
Daba mara	To halt; to rest; to encamp	Daba mara (threatened; imposed
Dabao (+M)	To press; to snub; keep under check	Dabao
Dabdaba (+M)	Broad; wide	Dabdaba (imposing influence)

Dabdub	To sink at once	Dubub; dubna
Dabi (K)	A small box or case; to lay claim to.	Datri
Dabi	Claim	Dawa
Dabkao (M)	To lie in wait; to crouch down in fear	Dabak ke
Dabot	To restrain; to forbid	
Dabri	To despise; threaten	
Dad (K)	Hard; hot tempered; strict	Dahda
Dad	Certain skin disease that does not break into sores	Dadri
Dada (M)	Elder brother	Pb. grandfather
Dada (R)	Ancestors; forefathers	Dada
Dada	Elder brother	Dada (grandfather)
Dadesko (R)	Paternal	Dadka
Daftri (K)	Book-binder	
Dag	Blemish	Dag
Dag; Jalao	Cremate	Dag
Dag; dagi (M)	Spot; blemish ; corruption	Dag; dagi
Daga (+M)	To deceive; misfortune	Daga
Dagabaj	Traitorous	Dagabaj
Dagabaz; dagabaji;	Traitorous;	Dagabaz

dagaboj (+M)	deceitful	
Dagao	To arrange for	Dagao
Dagar dagar (M)	Shaking of a large body	Dagar dagar
Dagar dagar	Quickly and with force	Dagar dagar
Dagi mara	Blemished	Dagi maria
Dagi	Branded	Dagi
Dagmagao	To shake	Dagmagao
Dagni(+M)	An iron with which the animals are marked	Dagni
Dah (+M)	Enmity	
Dahak (M)	Heat; flame	Dahakna
Dahar dahar; dahar dohor; duhur duhur	Quickly	Dahar dahar
Dahda Dumbar	Belongings; chattles	Dahda adumbar (Having large belongings)
Dahdahao	Hot; feverish	Dahdahao; dehkna
Dahgao	Blaze	Dahak
Dahi (M)	Curd	Dahi
Dahi	To claim	Dawa
Dahlao (M)	To shake; to quack	Dahlao
Dahna	A small quantity of grain given daily to an agrivultural laboror during harvest; over	

	and above his wages	
Dahoke	Envy; spite; malice	Dain
Dai (M)	Midwife	Dai
Dain (M)	A witch	Dain
Daini-dailko (K)	A witch	
Dak	post	dak
Dak-ora (M)	Post office	Dak-khana
Daka-daki (M)	To push one another	Dhaka dhaki
Dakdakao (M)	To burn with flame	Tamtamao ; jagmagao
Dakdalao	To shake	Dhaka dhaki
Dakh (M)	Vine; grape	Dakh
Dakh	A vine	Dakh
Dakhil (M)	To pay; to deposit	Dakhil
Dakhil	Arrive	Dakhal
Dakhila (M)	Receipt	Dakhila
Dakhila	A receipt for money paid	Dakhila
Dakhin (M)	South	Dakhan
Dakhir (K)	To deposit; entrust; file	Dakhil
Dakhna	The south	Dakhan
Dakhnahi	From the south	Dakni
Daktur	Doctor	Daktur
Daku (M)	Robber	Daku
Daku	A robber	Daku
Dal	To split into two like lentils	Dal
Dala (M)	Basket	Dala
Dala	A large	Dala

	basket	
Dalal (M)	A broker	Dalal
Dalal	Tout	Dalal
Dalali	Brokerage	Dalali
Dalan (M)	A mud or brick wall; a brick building	Urdu; courtyard
Daldal (M)	Marsh; swampy ground	Daldal
Daldalahi	Marsh	Daldal
Dalel	Documentary proof; argument	Dalel
Dali (M)	Pease; pulses split into two	Dali (dalna)
Dalidar (M)		Voracious
Dalil (M)	Document	Dalil (argument; thinking)
Dalkao (M)	To shake	Dalkao
Dalkao	To shake	Dalkao
Dallali	Brokerage fee	Dallali
Dalmal; dalmalao	To reverberate	Dilmil; dhamal
Dam (M)	Price	Dam
Dam dari	To fix prices	Dam dari
Dam	Wages	Dam
Dama (M)	Asthma	Dama
Dama	Asthama	Dama
Damadol (M)	To be in trouble; to be shaky	Danwandol
Dambri	One eighth of a pice	Damri
Damkam	Dues;	Damkam

	outstanding	
Damra (M)	An earthen lamp	Dewa
Damri (M)	Half price	Damri (usually; the smallest measure of money.
Dan (M)	Gift; alms	Dan
Dan	Gift	Dan
Dana (M)	Grain; gram	Dana
Dana Pani	Food and Drink	Dana Pani
Dana	Piece of grain	Dana
Danae; danai-ni (M)	To judge	Danae (wisdom)
Danai	To judge; deep understanding	Danai
Danapani (M)	Food and drink	Danapani
Dand (M)	Fine; punishment	Dand
Dand (R)	Tooth	Dand
Dand	Fine	Dand
Danda (K)	Deceiving; cheating; befooling	Dandi marna
Danda (M)	To be surprised	Dang
Danda;Jirbana	Fine	Dand;Jirmana
Dandalo; dandwala (R)	Having sharp teeth; Sharp toothed	Dandwala
Dandanao (M)	Quickly; to walk proudly	Dandanao
Dandanao	Quickly;	Dandanao

	furiously	
Dande (M)	To impose fine	Dande
Dandha (M)	Occupation	Dhanda
Dandha mandha	Uncertain; vaguely; doubtfully	Dandha mandha
Dandi (M)	A small stick; balance; device for small measurements like gold	Dandi `
Dandi	To be anxious	Dandi (marna); dhandli
Dang (K)	Yet; still; just	Dang (like in dang tapao)
Dang; dahang (M)	A long stick	Dang
Danga	To fight	Danga
Danga;Larai	Fight	Danga;Larai
Dangra; dangri (M)	Male and female servants	Dangra; dangri
Dangri	Cattle	Dangar
Dani	Liberal	Dani
Danoa (M)	Stick; club	Danda
Danra	An ox	Dand
Danta	A thick stick; a club	Danda
Dantao (M)	To rebuke	Dantna
Dao (M)	Opportunity; trick	Dao; da
Dao ghao	Opportunity; a good chance	Dao ghao
Dao	Opportunity	Dao

Daonri (M)	Cattle used for thrashing grain	*Seems derived from dand (bull)
Dapal (M)	A covering	Tarpal
Dapkao	To forbid; to subdue	Dabkao
Dar (M)	A line of raised earth for the purpose of sowing	Kiar
Dar dhup	To run hither and thither	Dor dhup
Dar	A rent; a price	Dar
Dara dar	Instantly; immediately	Dara dar
Dara	To come	Dara (passage through the hills)
Darako (R)	Fear; terror	Darako
Daral (R)	Be afraid; be terrified	Darakal
Daram	To show hospitality	Daram
Daram; dharam	Religion	Dharam
Daran	Steep	Dhalwan
Daran	To walk; to journey; to travel	Daran (Pb. birds' travel)
Darano (R)	Alarming; intimidating; fearful; frightening	Darau; darona
Darao (M)	To frighten	Darao
Darap (M)	Thing (meaning	Darab (Waris Shah)

	money)	
Daravel (R)	Terrifying; frightful	Dharvel (as dacoit seems related)
Darban	A door keeper	Darban
Darbar (M)	Meeting	Darbar
Darbar	A meeting	Darbar
Dardhup (M)	To run here and there	Durdhup
Darga	A precipice	Darga
Darha (+M)	A deep pool in a river	Darha
Dari (M)	To be able to; strength	Dari
Dari	rug	dari
Dariafat; dariap (M)	To enquire; to investigate	Dariafat
Darian	Sea or large river	Darian
Dariao (M)	Sea; ocean	Pb. river
Darilekha (M)	Fit; able	
Darja (+M)	Degree; rank	Darja
Darja	rank	darja
Darji (+M)	Taylor	Darzi
Darji	Tailor	Darji
Darkao (M)	To crack	Dakre hona
Darkhas	A petition	Darkhasat
Darokia	Afraid	Darakal
Darpoen (M)	A coward	Darpok
Darrao (M)	To grind pulses	Dalao; dalo
Darrao	To roll	Dhar lao
Daru (+M)	Gunpowder; liquor	Daru (Pb. medicine as well)
Daru	Liquor	Daru

Dasa; Dosa	Condition; state; luck	Dasa; wakha; disna; dakh
Dasa;Hal;Hawal;	Condition	Dasha; Hal;Hawal
Dasao; dhasao (+M)	To crumble; to collapse as a wall	Dhasna
Dasi	A female servant; a slave	Dasi
Dasna; dhasna	Slope of a hill	Dhalan
Dastur	Custom; usage	Dastur
Dat (K)	To beat	Dat; dant
Dat; data	A tooth	Dant; dand
Datani; dataone; datauni	A twig used as a tooth brush	Datani
Dati (M)	Tooth of sickle	Dati
Datra; Datura (M)	Dhutura plant	Dhutura
Datre	A small sickle	Datri
Datrisa	Bleeding from gums	Datrisa
Datrom	A toothed sickle	Datrom
Daulat	Wealth	Daulat
Daura	A large round shallow flat bottomed basket	Dala
Daura-dauri	Runing around	Daura-dauri
Dauraha	A village runner; guide or messenger	

Daw (K)	A cause; an excuse	Daw
Dawa (+K) (+M)	Claim	Dawa
Dawai (M)	Medicine	Dawai
Dawat; dowat;	Ink pot	Dawat
Daya	plaintively	daya
De	An interjection of entreaty	De
Deao (M)	To cause to give; to compel to pay	Deao; dewao
Debedebe	Staggering under weight	Debedebe
Deh	Body	Deh
Deh; dev; deva; dibi	An idol	Deva; but
Dehat (M)	Country	
Dehri (M)	Loan at 50% interest	
Dek (K)	A large cooking vessel	Deg
Deke	The hip	Dhas; dhase
Dekhao	View	Dekho
Dekhaoke; (+M) Dekhao	To be seen; to come into view	Dekhake
Dekhar (M)	To blech	Dekar
Dekhit	Deliberately; with eyes open	Dekhit
Del (R)	God; Supreme being	Dev
Del-khul	Cuss out; give	Gal dena

	shit	
Dem	Consistently; assiduously	Daim; Daem
Demer potom	Child by a former husband	Pichlag
Den	Giving	Den
Dendi (M)	Tailless; hairless; leafless	Dendi
Deo (M)	Deity; spirit	Deo
Deonra (M)	A witch finder; magician	
Deor (M)	Husband's younger brother	Deor
Der; deri (M)	Delay; to be late	Der; deri
Dera Deri	To put off time; being late	Dra deri
Dera	Camp	Dera
Derej (M)	Playfully; in a jocular manner	Deraj (patience)
Derhi (+M)	One and half	Derhi (Pb. two and a half)
Derza (R)	A rag	Darz; lir
Derzalo; derzalo; darzardyol; darzarel (R)	Rags; tattered; shredded	Derzan (variations of process of tattering)
Derzari (R)	Rag collector	Derzari
Derzi (R)	Rags tied to a tree; bush or	Derzi (old use of the word darzi as

	fence to show those following later which crossroad to take	tailor)
Des bides	One country after another	Des bides
Desh (R)	Ten	Das
Desh bresh (R)	A decade	Das baras
Desi	Native	Desi
Despoda	A wanderer; a vagrant	Desbhondo
Devel; devla	God	Dev
Devlaika (R)	Goddess	Devi
Dewa; sewa	Worship; service	Dewa sewa
Dewan (+M)	Prime minister; manager	Dewan
Dewani	Civil crime	Dewani
Dewtrai (K)	Solid earth	Dharti
Dha (M)	Sound of something falling	Dha
Dhaba	A verandah	Dhaba (roadside eatery)
Dhai	Mid wife	Dai
Dhak dhak	Flutter; throb	Dhak dhak
Dhak	Immediately; instantly	Dhak
Dhaka (+M)	To push	Dhaka
Dhaka dhaki	To push again and again	Dhaka dhaki
Dhakao (+M)	To cover; to obscure	Dhakao; dhakna

Dhakao	Cover	Dhak
Dhal (+M)	A shield	Dhal
Dhal	shield	dhal
Dham dhum	Noise	Dhum dhum
Dhamadhur (M)	Pompously	Dhamadhur
Dhamak; dhamas (M)	Influence	Dhamak
Dhamcul	Jolting	Dhamacukri
Dhamkao (+M)	To rebuke; to chide	Dhamkao (Pb. threaten)
Dhan;Daulat	Wealth	Dhan;Daulat
Dhandrau	To search for	Dhundh
Dhanga; dhangi (M)	Tall (male and female)	Dhanga; dhangi
Dhangar; Dhangaria	Rich; wealthy	Dhanwan
Dhani	An interjection; a term of endearment	Dhani
Dhania	Corriander	Dhania
Dhans dhons	To search here and there	Dhans dhons (Pb. imposition; counghing)
Dhap	Flame	Lat
Dhap dhapi	Stamping the foot	Dhap dhapi
Dhaper	Hurriedly	Dhapar
Dhar	Edge	Dhar
Dhara bandha	Against one's will; forcibly	Dhara Bandhi (Pb. to be divided into hostile groups)
Dhara dhari (+M)	Using violence	Dhara dhari
Dhara	section	dhara
Dharao (+M)	To apprehend;	Dharao

	to arrest; to be in debt	
Dharao	Apprehend	Dhar laina
Dharas (M)	Patience; beyond danger	Dharas
Dhari	Edge	Dhari (like do dhari talwar; it also mean an enclave amidist the tilled land; away from village; for residence and for keeping animals)
Dharmi (M)	Righteous; just	Dharmi
Dharna	A mode of extorting payment of a debt by making the person to sit in the sun or in any other way to making him uncomfortable; to sit till prayer is granted	Dharna (to sit in protest)
Dharpa (M)	Trap	Darba
Dharti (+M)	The world; the universe	Dharti
Dhas	To go in search of; to search	Dhas (Pb. & U hope Dharas)

Dhasao (M)	To collapse; to fall down; to pull down	Dhasao
Dhasau	To overcome; to conquer; to defeat	Dhans
Dhasna (M)	A pit; aa pit near the slope of a hill	
Dhat (+M) dhatu	A mineral; a metal	Dhat
Dhat	Metal	Dhat
Dhata	A stump of a tree	Dhata
Dhathi	Persistent; inexorable)	Dhathi
Dhathi	The stubble or stumps of crop left in ground at reaping time	Dhathi; mudh
Dhatin	To beat	Dhana
Dhatka (M)	Twig of a tree	Datin (to brush the teeth)
Dhatka	To deny; to disapprove	Dakan
Dhawa dhawi (+M)	Nearing the target to be attacked; to go in a large body	Dhawa
Dhawa	Attack	Dhava
Dhebua (M)	A piece; generally meaning two piece	Dhela

Dhela (M)	Clod of earth; a kind of thorny plant	Dhela; dhem
Dhelkusi (M)	A sling used to throw stones to a great distance	Ghulel (dhela suttan wali)
Dher (M)	A heap; many much	Dher
Dher	Much	Dher
Dhera (M)	A hand spindle	Muna?
Dherba; dhibri	Male and female who short in stature	Dhibri (Pb. A small screw).
Dhiaputa (M)	Family	Dhiput
Dhil (M)	Loose; to neglect	Dhil (to give free hand)
Dhil	Loose	Dhila
Dhilao (M)	Careless	Dhilla
Dhima (M)	Mild	Dhima
Dhinuk	Bow	Dhanush
Dhipni	A lid; a stopper	Capni
Dhiri; dheri (M)	A heap	Dheri
Dhirisusti (M)	Slowly	Susti
Dhirja	Contentment; patience	Dhirja
Dhirpur	To be fully contented	Bharpur
Dhit (M)	Obstinate; impudent	Dhit
Dhitai (M)	Impudence	Dhitai
Dhitao	Quarrelsome	Dhitao

Dhoka; dhokha (+M)	To deceive	Dhoka; dhokha
Dhokor; dhokora	A scornful negative	Dhotkar
Dhol (+M)	A drum	Dhol
Dhol;Dholki	Drum	Dhol;Dholki
Dholomolo (M)	Drowsy	Dhilmil
Dhon	Wealth; property	Dhan
Dhopso; dhoso	Lazy	Phosar
Dhorom	Religion	Dharam
Dhua	smoke	Dhuan
Dhuba; dhubi (M)	A small brass cup	Daba; dabi
Dhubi (+M)	Washerman	Dhubi
Dhuk dhuk (M)	To palpitate; to throb	Dhul dhuk
Dhuka	Hot; to be hot	Dhukhda
Dhukao	Bellows	Dhonkani
Dhukni	An unmarried woman who enters the house of the man of choice and thus compels him to marry her	
Dhulki (+M) dholki	A small drum beaten with fingers	Dhulki
Dhum (M)	Crowd	Dhum
Dhum; dhum dham	To bluster; tamasha	Dhum; dhum dham
Dhumur (M)	A kind of bee	Dhumuri
Dhumur-rasi	Honey of the	Dhumur chahad

	bee of Dhumur species	
Dhuna (M)	Smoke	Dhuna
Dhunao (M)	To card cotton	Dhunao
Dhund	Dim; indistinctly	Dhund
Dhundar	Smokey	Dhundar
Dhundra dhundri	To search here and there	Dhunda dhundi
Dhungia	Smokey	Duwankhia
Dhunia (M)	One who cards cotton	Dhunia
Dhup	Sunshine	Dhup
Dhup;offer	to;incense	Dhup
Dhur	Draught cattle; oxen or buffalos	Dhur (Pb. A person who is always made use of)
Dhurbaj	A rascal	Dhurbaj (Pb. Always making use of everyone
Dhurdhurao (M)	To hate; to drive out contemptuously	Dhurdhur
Dhuri (+M) dhur	Dust	Dhur+++++
Dhuri	Dust	Dhur
Dhurkara	An exclamation of annoyance or vexation	Dhurkara
Dhusa (+M)	A woolen blanket	Dhusa

Dhut (+M) dhoti	An exclamation of annoyance	Dhut
Dhuti	A cloth worn around the waist	Dhuti
Dhuá¹ꞌi	Dust	Dhur
Dia salai	Matches	Dia salai; machis
Dia; dimi (M)	Lamp	Dia
Die (K)	Betray; sell	Die
Digao (M)	To remove; to move	Digao; dego
Digmagao (M)	To shake	Digmigao
Digri	For English term decree	Digri
Dih; dhi; dehat	A village; a hamlet	Dih; dehat
Dihi (K)	Big and fat	Dihi (body)
Dikhimos (R)	Eyesight	Dikhi-mos (dekhan-monh)
Dikhitte	With open eyes; knowingly	Dekhte
Dil (M)	Mind	Dil
Dil	Courage; bravery	Dil
Dildal (M)	Swaying motion	Dhili dhali
Dili	A large basket in which grain is stored	Dili (Pb. gohla; gohlak)
Dili; dhili	To loosen; to slacken	Dili dhili
Dilkao (M)	To throw down by	Dilkao

	beating gently	
Dilman	Brave; plucky	Dilman (Pb. dilwala)
Dilwar (M)	Brave; bold	Dilawar
Dimak	Idle; unwilling; dull	Dimak (Pb. termite)
Dimak; dimaki (M)	Proud	Dimaki (arrogant)
Din	Day	Din
Din; dinta	A day	Din
Dina; dine	A future possibility	Dina (Pb. a future possibility of returning debt)
Dinam	Every day; daily	Dinam
Dinbhar (M)	Whole day	Dinbhar
Dinger	Poor	Dinger (Pb. Dangar is animal)
Dini	Give	Dini
Dinidar (+M)	Generous; liberal	Dindar (Pb. converted Muslim)
Dipa (M)	Mound; a raised ground	Tiba
Diri (M)	A stone	Dheli
Diri	Late	Diri
Disa (M)	Side; direction	Das; dicha
Disa	To remember; to have in mind	Disa
Dista; dit; jista	A quire of paper	Dasta
Disum (M)	Country	Des

Diuhe	A lamp	Diva
Diwano (R)	Conference; debate	Diwan
Djepo (R)	Pocket	Jaib; boja
Dkaw (K)	In reserve for an emergency	Dakia (hoia)
Do-pash-nango (R)	Half naked	Adh nanga
Do-pash-ryat	Midnight	Adh-rat
Doat (M)	Ink pot	Doat
Dobar (M)	Double; twice as much	Dobar
Dobe (M)	To dip in water	Dobe
Dobha (M)	Pond	Tobha
Dobka; Dopka	A basket used to lift water for irrigation	Boka (Pb. Tind)
Dobon	To lay an embargo on	Dobon
Dobrao (M)	To plough for the second time; to repeat	Dohar (ploughing)
Dodhari (M)	Double edged	Dodhari
Dog	A stain; to mark; brand	Dag
Doha-boha (M)	To carry away	Dhona
Dohanil (R)	Smoke	Dohwan
Dohao (M)	To cry for help	Dohai
Dohar	Double cloth	Dohar
Dohksew (K)	Dogged; obstinate	Dhakosala
Dohmat (M)	To blame	Tohmat
Dohra	To do a	Dohara; dobara

	second time	
Dohrao (M)	To double up; to plough for the second time	Dohar
Doja	Second growth second brew	Doja (Pb. only second)
Dokan (+M)	A shop	Dokan
Dokan	shop	dukan
Dokandar (M)	A shopkeeper	Dokandar
Dokha; dhokha (M)	To cheat; to disappoint; doubt	Dhokha
Dokhol (+M)	To occupy	Dokhol
Dokra (M)	Half price	Dakra (a piece)
Dol (+M)	An iron bucket for drawing the water from well	Dol
Dol-dal (M)	To stagger	Dol-dal
Dola	palki	dola
Dola; doli (+M)	A kind of Palki	Dola
Dolao (M)	To shake; to ring the bell	Dolao
Doloe-doloe	To walk with loosened hair in the wind	Dhola
Doloi (K)	A ruler or chief ; a title of honor	Dolai (like Dolai Lama)
Dolomolo	Sad looking	Dolomolo
Dom (+M)	A caste of aborigines;	Dom

	many of them are musicians	
Dom	To rest	Dam
Dombaj; dombaji	Deceiving	Dambazi
Domkao	Threaten	Damkao
Don (R)	The two of them; them both	Dono
Don	A wooden trough; for animals to eat or drink water	Pb. Daona means providing water to animals or taking them to water
Donbak (K)	To dare;	Dabang
Donde (R)	Between two; into two parts	Dopase
Dondho	Hazy; cloudy	Dondho
Dondo	Polled (ox or buffalo)	
Dongkor (K)	The back of the car	Digi
Dongo (R)	Jointly owned by both	Dosanjh
Donka	To publish scandalous statement to outcaste someone	Danka (Pb. Publicize)
Dopash (R)	Half	Do-khan; adha
Dopashil; dopashin (R)	To divide in half	Do-khan
Dophar	Layer over layer	Dophar
Dor (K)	Price	Dar

Dor bhao	Rate	Dar; bhah
Dora	Cord	Dora
Dorbar (K)	Coucil	Darbar
Dorbaria	One in the habit of attending dobors	Darbaria; darbari
Dorbin (K)	A telescope	Dorbimn
Dori (R)	Ribbon; lace; string	Dori (rasi)
Dorji (K)	A tailor	Darzi
Dorkhat (K)	A petition; an application	Darkhasat
Dormand; dormadi	Ailing; ill	Darmanda
Doro boro	Quickly	Doro boro (Pb. confused)
Dorobos (M)	All; ruin	Dabardos
Doroga (+K) (+M)	A head constable	Daroga; hawaldar
Dorokia	Fearful; timid	Drakal
Dorson	To see; to visit a sacred shrine	Darchan
Dorwan (K)	A doorkeeper	Darban
Doryavo (R)	River	Darya
Dos (+M)	Crime; panchayat	Dos (Pb. crime; fault)
Dos	Crime	Dos
Dos-lagau	To accuse	Dos-lagau
Dos;Galti	Fault	Dosh;Galti
Dosh (R)	Guilty; fault	Doch
Dosi;Opradi	Guilty	Doshi;Apradhi
Dosima	Boundry between two villages	Pb. bislane (Base line)
Dosket (K) (+M) doskhot	Signature	Dastkhat

Doskhot (K)	Signature	Daskhat
Dosra	second	doosra
Dostabit (K)	An agreement on paper	Dastawaiz
Doya (M)	Back; hinder part	Duhi
Duar (+K) (+M)	Enterance	Duar; darwaza
Duara	A house	Duara
Dub	Sink once for all	Dub (Pb. sink)
Duba; dubao (+M)	To flood; to cover with water	Duba
Dubi (K)	Washer man	Dhubi
Dud (K)	Milk	Dud
Dudul (M)	The act of pouring out	Dulna (Pb. dhudal is thick dust caused by continuous carts &.c)
Duhmot	To accuse falsely	Tuhmat
Duhri	Double	Duhri
Duito (R)	For the second time	Doja; doji
Duk; dukh (+M) duku	Sorrow; pain; grief	Dukh
Dukan (K)	A shop	Dukan
Dukandar (K)	A shopkeeper	Dukandar
Dukh (R)	Ache; agony; anguish; hurt; pain	Dukh
Dukh-ando-gi (R)	Bellyache	Dhid-pir
Dukha	To be in sorrow or	Dukhi

	anxiety	
Dukhali; dukhi	Suffering	Dukhali
Dul (+M)	To pour	Dul
Dular (+M)	To caress; to fondle	Dular
Dulara; dulari	Lover (male and female)	Dulara; dulari
Duli	A primitive type of Palki	Duli
Dulidar	A glutton	
Dumang (M)	A drum	Dumduma; dhol
Dumok (K)	To threaten	Dhamki
Dumur	A wild specie of honey bee	Dhmuri
Duna	Two fold	Duna
Dunal	The interjection of two rivers	Dunad
Dundge; dundgi	Bald; shaven head	Ganja; ganji
Dundrao (M)	To search about for anything	Dhundna
Dung (K)	To stab; pierce	Dung
Dunga (M)	To suspend; to hang; to carry by hanging	Tung; tang
Dunia (+M)	The world	Dunia
Dupal	To cover	Dupal
Dur (R)	Distant; far off	Dur
Dur dur	To reject; to put at a dstance	Dur dur

Durbin	optical instrument	durbin
Duria	A bunch of silk or cotton worn	Duria
Duriaw (K)	The sea	Darya (river)
Durshil (R)	Milk (cow)	Dudh
Durukia	Frightened	Daraku
Durust (+M)	To put in proper order	Durust
Dushmanil (R)	Making an enemy; enmity	Duchmani
Dusi	Guilty; blameworthy	Dusi; duchi
Dusko	Distress; trouble	Dusko (Pb. to cry in low tone)
Dusman (+K) (+M)	Enemy	Duchman
Dustama	Hatred; evil	Duchmani
Dustur (+K)	Custom; habit	Dastur
Duwai (K)	To pray	Duwa ; duaa
Duwares (R)	Twice	Do-wari
Dykyano (R)	Shop; store	Dukan
	E	
Ead	To remember; to memory	Yad
Eh	An interjection of surprise; O; what; indeed! Really!	Eh
Ehe to	So; thus	Ehe to

Ehe	Such as this	Ehe
Eit-nar (K)	Slag of an iron-furnace	Nar (ag)
Eitmut (K)	Nose pus	Sindh
Ejhar (+M)	A statement made before a magistrate	Ezhar
Ejlas; Ijlas (+M)	A court of justice	Ijlas (Pb. meeting; large gathering.
Ejmal (M)	Joint	Miljul; jumal (Jumal jahan; Mian Muhammad Bhakash)
Ek Sath	United	Ekath
Ek jeba	Fearless; Only oneself to care for	Ek jeba
Ek sath (+M)	United	Ek sath
Ek sirri	Self-willed; obstinate	Ek sirri
Eka (+M)	One; alone	Eka
Eka duka	One or two; a few	Eka duka
Eka eki	One by one	Eka eki
Ekaha	Alone; without a mate	Ekaha; kalla
Ekam	one	ekam
Ekamoe	United; of one mind	Ekamohin; Ekmonh; yak zaban
Ekan; ekant	Privately; alone; solitary	Ekant; ekan

Ekarha	Alone; odd; one layered or dimension	Ekarha
Ekat; ekot	Privately	Ekant
Ekbar; Ekbargi (+M)	All at once; completely	Entirely
Ekbhakia	Only one word	Ekbhachia
Ekdhar	One side; aside; egde	Ekdhar
Ekh; yekh (R)	One	Ik
Ekhe-thanes	Together	Ik-than
Eklak	To become alone	Elag
Ekrar (+M)	To promise	Ekrar
Ekrar;Kabul	Confess	Kabul
Ektiar; Ektiari; (+M)	Authority	Ekhtiar
Ektorpha (M)	One sided	Ektarpha
Elaka (M)	Country; province	
Elaka	Province; district; area	Elaka
Elaka;Jila	District	Elaka;Jila
Enc	Now	Enj
Ence	To dance	Nece
End	The male organ of generation	Lend
Engatepo (M)	Thumb	Angotha
Enko; inko	Those	Unko
Eno	Now	Hun
Ente	In that way	Etran; otran
Era; erat	Wife; female	Aurat
Erpher	To alternate	Erphar
Esel	Fair; light colored	Esel (Pb. pure)

Etbar (+M)	Trustworthin ess	Etbar
Ete (+M)	There	Ethe
Eto	So much	Etna
Ezero (R)	One thousand	Hazar
	F	
Fanari (R)	Lamp	Fanos
Faravono (R)	Pharaoh	Faraon
Farsikanitsko (R)	Persian	Farsi
Farsiya (R)	Persian (person)	Farsiya
	G	
G	Nephew	Bhatija
Ga	A village	Gaon
Gabar	Mixed	
Gabha (+M)	The middle	Gabha; Gabhla
Gabha	Centre	Gabha
Gabhand	The ear formed within the sheath	Guluband
Gabhin	Pregnanat	Gabhin
Gabre	To take stealthily	Garbar
Gachi (+M)	A seeding after it has been pulled up for transplantati on	Gaci
Gad	Deep	Gad (buried deep)
Gad	The scum	Gad; mail

	which rises to the surface of sugar juice when being boiled	
Gada	A heap	Gada (A big pillow to put behind while sitting down)
Gada	Trench	Gada
Gada; garha	A hole; a pit	Gada (Pb. A cart)
Gadao	Bury To	Gadna
Gadar (+M)	Nearly ripe	Gadra
Gadbad	Confused	Garbar
Gadbe	To muddle	Gadla
Gadha (+M)	A donkey	Gadha; khota
Gadha	Donkey	Gadha
Gadha-godho	Up and down	Godna; godi
Gadhi	She donkey	Gadhi; khoti
Gadhra	Thick and unwholesome	Gadla
Gadi	Cart	Gadi
Gadiau	To sink; to bury	Gadna
Gadla (+M)	Thick; muddy and unclean	Gadla
Gador	Disobedient; obstinate	Gadr
Gaela gaela	Indistinct	Gela
Gagar (M)	The quail	Titar
Gagar;Ghara	Waterpot	Gagar;Gharda
Gagra (+M)	A brass water pot	Gagra
Gahak	Buyer	Gahak
Gahak; gahki; gohrak	A buyer	Gahak

Gahan	Eclipse	Grahan
Gahana	An eclipse of sun or moon	Gahana; garahan
Gahna (M)	An ornament	Gana
Gahri	Long continued and severe	Gahri
Gai	Cow	Gaan
Gaj (+M)	A measuring rod	Gaz
Gaj	Measuring Rod	Gaj
Gaji	A narrow piece of cloth about one cubit in breadth and any length	Gaji
Gakhur	Proficient; efficient	Gakhia
Gal goppo	Gossip	Gal goppo
Gal	To speak; to boast; to brag	Gal
Gala	Voice	Gala (throat)
Galao (+M)	To melt	Galao
Galao	Decompose	Galna
Galat Solat	Unintelligible	Galat salat
Galbajri	Talkative	Galbatia; galhri
Galgalao	To make a noise; to make a row; din or tumult	Galgalao
Gali (M)	To abuse	Gali
Galsal	Converrse	Galshal
Galti	A slip; a fault	Galti
Galua	A boaster; a	

	braggart	
Gama (M)	Affixed to	Jama; jura
Gambhir (+M)	Serious; good natured; grave	Gambhir
Gambhra gada	The pit in which the fire is placed when boiling gur	Cumba
Gamhand	Haughtiness; arrogance	Gamhand
Gan	Properly; suitable	Gan
Gandaura	Rubbish; rubbish in heap	
Gande munde	Dirty	Gunde munde
Gandhak (+M)	Sulphur	Gandhak
Gandi Gandic	A term of abuse	Gandi
Ganga (+M)	The river of Ganges	Ganga
Ganga gaya	To perform the last rites of the dead	Ganga gaya
Ganga tulsi	A common plant with a pleasant smell	Tulsi
Ganga	Ganges	Ganga
Gangun	Having impediment in speech; dumb	Gunga
Ganja ganji	Overcrowded	Pb. Ganja; ganji

	; to break and mix	two villages in Gurdaspur; East Punjab; India; word â€˜gunjan' may be derived from this
Ganja; ganjao (M)	Hemp; to hep up	Ganj (collected heap)
Ganjao	To mix up	Ganjao
Gano garib	Very poor	At garib
Ganti (M)	To stir up with a spoon while cooking	Ghotna
Ganti	To count	Ginti
Gao (M)	Wound	Gao
Gaowar (+M) Gonwar	Foolish	Gawar
Gap sap (M)	Talk	Gap chap
Gap	Prolixity; rumor	Gap
Gaphlat (M)	Negligence	Gaphlat
Gaphlat; gaphil	Negligence; neglect; fault	Gaphlat
Gapi (+M)	Gosper	Gapi
Gar (M)	Fort	Garh
Gar;mahal	palace	mahal
Gara	Trouble; danger	Gara
Garad (M)	Jail	Garad (a group of soldiers appointed to keep control of someone)
Garah	A pitcher	Garah
Garaj; Sud	Interest	Garaj; Sud
Garaj; goroj	Concern; necessity;	Garaz

	want;need	
Garbar; garbarao (+M)	Confuse; mixing up	Garbar; garbarao
Garda (+M)	Dust	Garda
Gardan (+M)	The neck	Gardan
Gardan	Neck	Gardan
Gargar	Sound of gurgling or hubbling	Gargar
Garh	A fort; residence of a Zemindar	Garh (Pb. house; residence)
Garha (M)	A water channel	Khala
Garha-gorho (M)	Full of pits	Gadhe; toey
Garhao	To make; to give shape	Garhao
Garia	Doer or agent	Gar (like bazi gar)
Garib (M)	Poor	Garib
Garib mara	To kill the poor; to oppress	Garib mari
Garja garji	To howl	Garja garji
Garjao (+M)	To growl	Garjao
Garma garmi	To become heated; heated discussion	Garma garmi
Garmao	To become heated; to warm	Garmao
Garosti	Household; family	Garasti
Garosti;Ghar Gusti	Family	Gharasthi
Garsande	A stand for water pots	Garwanje

Gasao	To rub	Gasao
Gasar (M)	To clean utensils by rubbing	Ghasana
Gasen	Amidst; amongst	Ghusia
Gasrao	To drag	Gasitna
Gathia	Short of stature but youthful appearance	Gathia (Pb. githa is short but guthia is youthful)
Gati (M)	Relative; friend; companion	Sangti
Gav; gava (R)	A village; small town	Gaon
Gavari (R)	Rural inhabitant; villager	Gavar
Gavutuno (R)	Farmer; peasant	
Gawao	To loose; to injure	Gawao
Gayum	To finish; all; whole	Gayum (Pb. gone)
Geda; gedi	Short male and female	Githa; githi
Gegran	To grown; to beg hard and helplessly	Gergran
Gejet	Gazette; a newspaper	Gezat
Gend (+M) genda	A ball	Gend
Gendher	To move while in a sitting	Gesitna

	position the hands being employed to propel the body	
Gendlan	Small	Gendlan (like the mustard gendlan)
Genthe	Knotty	Gendh; ganth
Gestaha; gestahi	Dirty; filthy; untidy	Ghatia
Ghag	Center of a river or tank	
Ghagra	A brass water pot	Ghagra
Ghal	To wound; to subdue	Ghael
Ghamandi	To boast; arrogant	Ghamandi
Ghangri	A loosely woven cloth ; a skirt worn by little girls	Ghagri
Ghani (+M)	One time amount of raw material put in an oil press	Ghani
Ghanta (+M)	An hour; a bell	Ghanta
Ghanta;Ghari	Clock	Ghanta;Ghari
Ghanti (+M)	A small bell	Ghanti
Ghao (+M)	A wound	Ghao
Ghao	Cut	Ghao
Ghao;Jakham	Wound	Ghao;Jakham
Ghar gusti	Household	Ghargrasti
Ghar	Strait;	

	difficulty	
Ghar-dijoa (M)	A son-in-law who is adopted by the family of the bride	Ghar-jawai
Gharaia; gharana	Belonging to a family	Gharana
Gharana	Household	Gharana
Ghari (+M)	A space of time; a time piece	Ghari
Ghari	Watch	Ghardi
Ghari-kade (M)	A little while	Gari-pal
Ghari;Polok	Instant	Ghari;Pal
Gharwa	A sparrow	
Ghas	Grass	Ghas; ghah
Ghasa Ghasi	Rubbing	Ghasa ghasi
Ghasao	scrap;to	ghasao
Ghasiara	Grass cutter	Ghasiara
Ghaskao (+M)	To sulk from the work; to escape; to slip away	Khisku
Ghaskao	To push or move along the ground	Khaskao; ghasito
Ghat (M)	An elevated range	Ghat (as of river)
Ghat	A way down to a river; a difficult pass through hills; opportunity; way of exit	Ghat
Ghatal-barhal (M)	Loss and	Ghata-wadha

	profit	
Ghatao (+M)	To reduce; to become less	Ghatao
Ghatao	Decrease	Ghatana
Ghatdar	A person in charge of a toll	Ghatdar
Ghate ghat	At each pass	Ghate ghat
Ghati (+M)	A shortcoming; loss	Ghati
Ghati barhi	Decrease and increase	Ghata wadha
Ghati	Loss	Ghata
Ghatna	Event	Ghatna
Ghatwar (M)	A watchman on a ghat	Ghatwar
Ghawar	To fence	Ghawar (Ghar war)
Ghej mej	To confuse; to mix	Ghec mec
Gheje beje	Without symmetry; anyhow	
Gherao	Encircle	Ghera
Ghin	Disgust	Ghin
Ghinao (M)	To hate	Ghinaona
Ghitli	Short in stature	Githi
Ghogo	Big strong voice	Ghogo; ghugu
Gholta ghulti	To roll in the dust	Ghatio ghati
Ghor bagi	A gig or any wheeled conveyance	Ghora bagi

	drawn by horses	
Ghor ghusia	One who stays in the house; idler	Ghar Ghusia
Ghorna (+M)	A fence; to fence round	Ghorna (Pb. a narrow corner or a hole)
Ghotna; Ghotona	An event; an occurrence	Ghatna
Ghulghul (M)	Darkness caused by clouds	Ghanghur
Ghunghura (M)	Ankle bell	Ghunghro
Ghurant (M)	Circuitous	Ghum-chakar
Ghuri ghuri	Time after time	Ghari ghari
Ghus (+M)	Bribe	Ghus
Ghus; Risbod	Bribe	Ghus;Rishvat
Ghusa (+M)	To prod with the thumb passed between the fore and middle finger	Ghusa; hura
Ghusao (M)	To cause to penetrate	Ghusao
Ghusau; gusan	To hide with a wish to shirk work; to loose an opportunity	Ghusau; gusan (Ghus may have been derived from it).
Ghutla; Ghutli	Short in structure	Githa; githi
Ghutni	To mesh up dal etc	Ghutni

Gian	Knowledge	Gian
Gichil (R)	Guess; estimate	Giwir
Gidi (+M)	Vulture	Gidh
Gidi	Vulture	Gidh
Gila (+M)	Moist	Gila
Gila	Humid	Gila
Gilas (+M)	A brass drinking vessel in shape of a tumbler	Gilas
Gilthi (+M) gilti	A swelling in the groin	Gilti
Gin (R)	Count	Gin
Gindo/gundo (R)	Assumption; consideration; feeling; idea; impression; intention; opinion; plan; theory; thought; suggestion	Gin-na
Gindol (R)	Have a thought; be thinking	Ginin
Gindosko (R)	Thoughtful; Well founded; thought out	Ginia-mithia
Gindyol (R)	Be counted	Gino
Ginel (R)	Add; count	Ginti
Ginti	Count	Ginti
Gira	Knot	Gira

Giri (M)	To fall down; to throw away	Giri
Girja (+M)	To join or conduct a religious service; church	Girja
Giru (M)	Red earth	Giru
Gitak	A thin film believed to be on the underside of a child's tongue at birth; which if not removed affects his speaking ability; an impediment in the speech	Gitak (Pb. kernel or seed of a fruit)
Giv (R)	Grain; corn; wheat	Gihon
Glaba (R)	To impose a fine; fine	Galba (to impose)
Goa (M)	Witness	Gwah
Goala; goar	A cow keeper	Goala
Gob	To steel; to put out of the way	Gaib
Gobaro	Manure	Gobar;Goha
Gobraha (M)	Dirty; unclean	Ganda
Gobrao	Manure; cattle manure	Gohia; gobar

Gocha	To hold in the lap	Good
Gode (M)	To pluck	Godna (godi karna)
Godhro	Thick; dull	Godha; gudha
Goetha (M)	Dried cow dung	Goea (pathian)
Goetha	Cow Dung	Goha
Goha	Witness	Gavah
Gohom (M)	Wheat	Gaiho; kanak
Goja	A mixture of Indian corn and rice cooked together	Pb. Gotawa; mixed bhosa with cotton seeds made for precious/milk giving animals. Its root may go back to gao (cow).
Goke	To carry on shoulder; to promise	Pb. goka means the milk or ghee of cow
Gol (+M)	Round; circular	Gol
Gol	spherical	gol
Gola	Throat	Gala
Gole (M)	To whistle	Gole
Golumbo (R)	A dove	Ghughi
Gomosta	An agent	gomachta
Gon	To give a daughter in marraige	
Gongha; Ghunga	The shell of water	Gongha
Gop; gopao	To hide; to keep back; to	Gop; gopao

	suppress; to keep secrete	
Gop;Gupat	Hide	Gupat
Gopca	A method of carrying small articles tied up in a cloth swung over the shoulder	Bogca
Goppo	Gossip	Gap
Gor (R)	Border; brink; edge; end; extremity; limit; out limit; tip	Gor (grave but not in Roma)
Gora (+M)	European ; fair	Gora
Gora	The refuse of matkom from which liquor has been distilled	Goda; guda
Gorji	Need; want; necessity	Garz
Gorla; gurli	Stripd as a tiger	Gorila
Gorob	The foetus	Gharab (pregnant)
Gorobia	Proud; conceited; fastidious	Gorab; garb (garb gahiliay ni; Waris Shah)
Gorom	Hot	Garam
Goso (M)	To wither; to anoint	Ghus (gawac)
Got; goth; gothao (+M) goth	Where cattle are collected	

	at mid-day	
Gotao	To thread; to string	Gota (women stich colorful strips to their cloth; gota kinari)
Gotom (M)	Clarified ghee	Ghee
Grasni (R)	Mare; battle-axe	Ghori; khacar
Gripdar	Arrest	Griftar
Gua	The Areca nut	Gua
Gubli	A small bag; a beggar's wallet	
Gubri	The contents of the stomach of a sheep or goat	Gubar
Gucan	To finish; to destroy	Gucan
Guci	Small bundle	Gatha
Gudi	Kite	Gudi
Guhum	Wheat	Gaihun
Guja	A wedge	Killa; khunta
Gujran	To pass as a time	Guzran
Gujur;Miritik;Morna	Death	Gujarna;Mritik;Marna
Gulako (R)	Round loaf of a bread	Guli (in western Punjab; roti is called guli as well)
Gulam	slave	gulam
Gulash (R)	Meat stew	Gulash
Guli (+M)	A ball; shot	Pb. Small wood piece sharpened

		from both ends to play with stick; danda. Game is guli danda).
Gulmal (+M)	Fusion; confusion; noise	Gulmal
Gumasta	Agent	Gumashta
Gun	Virtue	Gun
Guna (+M)	Sin; crime	Guna
Gunagar	Crime; the penalty	Pb. Sinner; criminal
Gunan	Multiply	Gunan
Gund	To ponder; to think over	
Gundi	To think deeply over; hidden meaning	Gundhi
Gunga (M)	Dumb	Gunga
Gunha;pap	sin	gunah;pap
Guni	Secrecy	Pb. Person with gun
Gunoi (R)	Garbage; trash; rubbish	Goon (human excrement)
Gunthi	Knee	Goda
Gupat; Gupti	To hide; to conceal	Gupt
Gupi (M)	To graze cattle	Gupi
Gur (+M)	Raw sugar	Gur
Gur	Crystalized Raw Sugar	Gur
Gura (M)	Abscess	Phura
Gurakhul	Tobacco mixed with	

	gur	
Gurmuchao (M)	To twist	Ghumao
Gurmuria	Round; spherical	Gol
Guru (+M)	A teacher; a leader	Guru
Guru	Teacher	Guru
Gut	Total	Gut (Pb. To brad and pony tail hair).
Gutri	Family; stock	Gut
Gutu	To thread as a needle; to string as beads	Gundho; Prona; Wainana
Gyanta (R)	Gum	Gund
H		
Habadia	A glutton; to eat greedily	Habaria
Had	Bone	Had
Hada (M)	A bullock	Dhaga; dangar
Hadeto (R)	Custom; habit; tradition; traditional value	Hadait; adit
Hae; hae	An exclamation of sorrow	Hae
Hahakar	Consternation; lamentation; wilderness; desert	Hahakar
Hai	Yes	Han

Haikat (M)	To wonder; to marvel; to be amazed	Hairat
Hajam (M)	A barber	Hajam; nai
Hajam	To digest	Hazam
Hajam;Pacao	Digest	Hajam;Pachao
Hajan (K)	Near	Je-ja; hethe
Hajar (+K) Hajir (+M)	Present	Hazar
Hajar (K)	One thousand	Hazar
Hajrao	Face to face	Hajrao
Hajri (M)	Attendance	Hazri
Hajri	Attendance	Hajri
Hajur (+M)	A respectful form of address; sir	Hazur
Hak hak	To laugh	Has has
Hak nahak (+K)	Without cause or reason	Hak nahak
Hak	To call to cattle when driving them	Hak (Pb. calling anyone)
Hak; hok (+M)	Right	Hak
Haka-baka; aka-baka (M)	To be surprised; to wonder; to be taken aback	Haka-baka
Hakao (M)	To call; to cry out	Kaik marna; kuk marna
Hakao	To call or shout out to bid at an auction	Hakao; Boli dena
Hakim (+K) (+M)	A magistrate	Hakim (Pb. ruler)

Hal (+M)	Moisture; sap	Hal
Hal boha	A ploughman	Hal waha; hali
Hal cal (+M)	News; intelligence	Hal cal
Hal; Halat; hal ahwal	Condition; state; circumstance	Hal; Halat
Hal;Halat	Circumstances	Hal; Halat
Halahalao	To press; to hurry	Halhalao
Halap (+M)	An oath; solemn affirmation	Halaph
Halap kasam	oath	Kasam
Halbal (+M)	Restless	Halcal
Hale	For now; under the circumstances	Hale
Haler	To ruin or destroy crops by grazing on them	Haner
Halhal	Urgent	Halhal
Hali (K)	An irrigated rice field; a set of four things	Hali (Pb. ploughman)
Hali sali	A short time ago; for the time being	Hal sal
Halka	Slight; to think lightly of	Halka
Halkao	To envy; to	Halka

	yearn for what others have	
Halla (+M)	Bravo; noise; uproar	Halla
Halla	Encourageme nt	Halla
Haluman (M)	Black-faced monkey	Hanuman
Halwae (+M)	Sweet meet maker and seller	Halwae
Hamal (+M) hambal	Heavy; burdensome; pregnant	Hamal (Hamla is a pregnant woman)
Hamal khun	To cause an abortion	Hamal digna (dagana)
Hamsaia (K)	Neighbors	Hamsaia
Hana (K)	So they say; it is said that	Hana
Handa (M)	A big earthen pot	Handi (earthen pot to cook)
Hane	Yonder; away over there	Hane (like in Hane bane)
Hangam (+M) hangama	To riot; to rebel	Hangam
Hani	Harm	Hani
Hantao	To rebuke; to chide	Hatak
Hapho	To pant; to breath heavily	Hapho
Hapsi Duke	Asthma	Sah dukh
Hapta (+M)	A week; a week's wage	Hafta
Hapta	Week	Hafta

Har-waha	Ploughman	Hali; hal-wahan
Haram (M)	Old; to become old	Haram (forbidden)
Haran; haron	Confusion; bother	Heran (astonished)
Harana Morna	To die a natural death	Marna
Harao (+M)	To conquer; to defeat	Harao
Harao	Conquer	Harana
Harapo/Xarapo	Dark skinned; giant cannibal orge in folk tales	Harapo (seems dark-skinned people in Punjab were called such. Word's relationship to Harappa is difficult to establish)
Harbarao; Harbar	To rumble or roll; thunder	Harbarao
Harek	Everyone	Harek
Hariar (+M)	Green	Hara
Harkat; Harket		Pb. movement
Harkhao	To wish what other have	Hirakh
Harkhetia	Miserable; troubled; wretched	Harya (Pb. defeated one)
Harna	Deer	Hiran
Harop (+M)	A letter of the alphabet	Haraph
Harrap; Hadrap	Fradulent; overreaching ; as a moneylender	Harap (Pb. swallow)

	cheating his debtors; harsh	
Harumbash (R)	Bandit leader; male bandit; usually applied to those who commit armed robbery with violence	Badmach
Harwaha	A ploughman	Hali
Has	Glee	Has
Has; hasi; hasi tamasa	Pleasure; delight; joy	Has
Hasae khelae	Fun; frolic; gleeful	Hasae khelae
Hasi kusi (+M)	Jubilant; rejoicing; in high spirit	Hasi khushi
Hasi thatta	Joking; fun; jesting	Hasi thatta
Hasi	A metal ornament worn round the neck	Hasi
Hasil	Get	Hasil
Hasli ghao	A sore on the neck	Hasli ghao
Hasna; hasanua	To joke; to make fun	Hasna; hasana
Hasuru (M)	To cease raining	Husar
Hat (K) (+M)	A market	Hut

Hat chut; hat cut; hat cuti	Active; energetic; skillful; quick in movement	Hat chut (Pb. A person keen to get into fight or hitting)
Hat; hatia	A moveable market; a market held at intervals; of a week	Hat; hati (Pb. shop)
Hata badi	To vie; to contest; rivalry	Hat jori
Hatai (R)	Rights	Hak
Hatao (M)	To cause to recede; to separate	Hatao
Hatao	To push back or away	Hatao
Hataori (+M)	A hammer	Hatori
Hatar (M)	To hang a child on the back by wrapping it up with cloth	Kandhar
Hatbajar	Market with shops	Hatbazar
Hathado (R)	Cheated; conned; deceived; a victim of fraud	Hath hona; hath ho jana
Hathi (+K) Hati	An elephant	Hathi
Hathi	Clamorous; persistent; headstrong	Dhati
Hathiar	Instrument	Hathiar

Hatiar	Implement	Hathiar
Hatiau; hathiao	To take; to lay hands on;	Hathiau
Hatkao	To be repulsed; to be driven back	Hatkao
Hatkari (+K) (+M)	Handcuffs	Hathkari
Hatu (M)	From the village	Hatu
Hatya	Weak; emaciated	Hina
Haya (+M)	To wish; to desire	Haya
He; hehe	Yes; to admit	He
Hebajot	To take care of; to preserve; to defend; to protect; to guard	Hefazat
Hej	Disrespectfully; tauntingly; disparagingly	Hez (Pb. hej means yearning for someone; the felling of closeness)
Heke	Right; just	Heke; haq te
Hela	To neglect; negligently; carelessly	Hela (Pb. excuse; to find a way to do something)
Helao (+M)	To move on	Helao
Helmel (M)	Friendly	Halem
Hena	To exist	Hona
Henla	Poor; ignorant	Hena
Her (K)	To fly;	Her (character of

	awfully; exceedingly	folklore); hor
Heran	Surprisingly; intensely	Heran
Here phere; ghuri phiri	Time after time; frequently	Here phere (Pb. also means deceiving)
Hergela (R)	Herd; drove; string	Harjela (havoc of partition was called harjela i.e. people moved in droves
Hesalia	Envious; spiteful	Hasid
Hesece sekrece	To be merry; to enjoy oneself	Hase khede
Hesrao	To pant; to breath heavily because of bronchitis	Hesaro (Pb. hussar lagna)
Het	Low; low down	Heth
Hetet	To provoke; to annoy	Hetet
Hia	Love; fondness; liking; longing	Hia
Hicha	Wish; desire	Hichia; Ichia; icha
Hichi	Hiccup	Hicki; hitki
Hifta; ifta (R)	Seven	Hafta (from Persian haftam)
Hiftao (R)	Seventh	Hafte
Hih (K)	Yes	Hei
Hikmat	Wisdom	Hikmat

Hilau	To move; to shake	Hilau
Hilmil	Friendly; on good terms with each other	Hilmil (it can be hilimi meaning softly; patiently)
Hin	Low deficient; weak	Hin (root word for hina)
Hina	That; that one	Hinan
Hindol	revolving	hindol
Hinjrau	To mourn; to lament; to sorrow over	Hinjrau (from Pb. word hanju meaning tears)
Hint	Ishara	
Hir (M)	To fan	Hir
Hir	Rice land reclaimed by throwing a dam across a stream or nala	Hir
Hira (+K) (+M)	A diamond	Hira
Hira	Diamond	Hira
Hiran (K)	Tired	Hiran; thakna
Hirdani	Sorrow; to grieve; mourning	Hirdani (from hirda)
Hirkha	Aversion	Hirkh
Hirohi	To long for; to sigh for; to crave for	Hirsi; hirakh
Hirom; Hiromea	Co wives	Haram
His; hisa (+K)	Share; portion; part;	Hisa

	division	
Hisab	Account	Hisab
Hisab; Lekha Jokha	Account	Lekha; Hisab
Hit Prit	Affection	Preet
Hit pirit; hit mitar (+M) hiriti; pirti	Friendship; love; affection	ZHZip pirit; hit mitar
Hoe; Hoyok; Hoyuk	To be; to become; to come into existence; to suffice; to happen; to come to an end	Hoe; howan; pura howan
Hojore	Quickly	
Hok (K)	Right; justice; uprightly	Hak
Holon	To grind into flour or meal; to grind to powder	Holon (round havan is used for pressing and mixing).
Hon-hon (K)	Like flour which has been mixed with water	Taon
Honatak; Hona	That one	Honan
Hor bara	To grow; to increase	Hor bara
Hora	A line; a section	Hora
Hore	An exclamation of surprise	Hore; khowre
Hormo	To be pregnant	Hamla

Hormot (K)	Chastity; honor	Hurmat
Hos (+M)	Consciousness	Hoch
Hoyo (M)	Air; wind	Hawa
Hu	To express assent	Hu
Hub	Pleasure; enjoyment; freedom from care	Hub (love; attachment)
Huiya; Huiyate	Being; an unexpected occurrence	Huiya; Huni; hooni
Hujat (+M)	To annoy; to bother	Hujat (Pb. making fun of)
Hujuk hujuk	In crowds; from all sides	Hujum
Huka	Hubble Bubble	Huka
Hukar (M)	A low moan or growl; a cry of a buffalo	Hukar (to produce loud voices to scare away the birds from newly sown fields or fruit trees)
Hukum (+M)	An order	Hukum
Hukum	order	hukam
Hul	To riot; to rebel	Hul
Hulmal	Riot; disturbance; mutiny	Hurmar
Hun mente	Immediately; quickly	Hune hune

Hunar	Industrious	Hunar (know how; being adept in some art)
Hungyal (R)	Creak; groan; moan	Hangura
Hur hur (K)	Very; an over-ripe fruit	Hur hur
Hurka; hurkar (+M)	A wooden bar for a door	Hura
Husiar (+M)	Intelligent	Huchiar
Husiar	sly	husiar
Husnak	Beautiful	Husnak
Hut	Strong headed; self willed	Hut
Hyndai (K)	In old times	Handai; handia (wela)
Hynne (K)	A short time ago	Hune
	I	
Iaka (K)	To make friends or join	Iaka
Ialado (K)	Self; to one self	Ilahida
Ialap (K)	To say; to preach	Ialap; ilana
Iasam (K)	To bathe	Achnan
Iate	Through; by means of; owing to	Iste
Idi	Heel	Adi
Ih; ish	A cry caused by sudden	Ih

	pain or clod	
Ijar (K)	To report to the authority	Araz
Ijara (+M)	A farming lease; a privilege; income of variable amount let for a fixed sum	Ijara
Ijara pata	A lease of land	Ijara pata
Ijaradar (+M)	A farmer of land and revenue	Ijaradar
Ijaradari	Farming or contracting for rent or revenue	Ijaradari
Ijhahar; ijhar	A deposition; statement or evidence given in a court	Izhar; bian
Ijot (K)	Reputation; honor	Izzat
Ijra (K)	A long term lease	Ijra (from jari karna)
Ikrar nama	A wriiten agreement; bond or contract	Ikrar nama
Ikrar	To promise; to pledge	Ikrar
Iktiar; iktiari (+K)	Power; authority	Ikhtiar

Ilaka (+M)	Area; jurisdiction	Ilaka
Ilaka (K)	District; area	Ilaka
Ilaka	province	ilaka
Ilam	Knowledge	Ilam
Imam-baksis	Reward	Inam-bakhchich
Iman (+M)	Belief; faithful; trustworthy	Iman
Iman (K)	Regard; respect	Iman
Imandar (+M)	Faithful; honest believer	Imandar
Imtihan (M)	Examination	Imtihan
In gan; in gante; in gonte	Reasonable; moderately; within compass	
In; inak	So much; so many	Inak
Inchi (+M)	Cor. Of English word inch; 1/12 of a foot	Inchi
Indara	A well	
Ine (K)	This	Ine
Ine	I	Ine
Ing (K)	To be burnt; to catch fire	Cinang
Ing-dara (K)	A temporary shed; tent	Dhara
Ing-kirja (K)	A church. A chapel	Girja
Ing-paki (K)	A house with stone walls	Paka (makan)

	and concrete ceiling	
Ino (K)	Which	Ehno
Inspetar	Cor. English; inspector	Inspector
Inta (M)	Brick	It; ient
Inya (R)	Nine	Nun
Ioh-mon (K)	To get to do one's own will	Man-marzi
Iong-rein (K)	Dusk; evening	Rein is rain; night
Iriang (K)	Passionate; irritable	Irngna; iring
Isa (+M)	Christ	Isa
Isai (+M)	Christian	Isai
Isara		
Isbis	To be irritated; provoked	Isbis
Isko	So; this	Isko
Isor (+M)	God	Ishwar
Isor	God	Isar
Ispang	Cor; English sponge	Ispanj
Ispat (M)	Steel	Dhat
Istapha (M)	Surrender; resignation	Istipha
Isthir	Quite; still; settled	Ashtar
Istihar (+M)	Notice; proclamation	Ichtiar; ichtihar
Istihar	Notice	Ishtihar
Istri	An iron	Istri
Iswi (+M)	Christian	Iswi
It (K) (+M) ita	A brick	It

Ita	Seed	
Itbar; itwar	Trustworthin ess	Itbar
Ithas (+M)	History	Ithas
Iti	This; this present	Iti; eh
Iw-sieng (K)	To have a pungent sniffy smell	Iw is smelling but sieng is the same as sungh in Punjabi
Iyo	So; this; as	iyo
	J	
Jab	When	Jab
Jabab; jabob (+M)	Answer	Jwab
Jabid	To attach under a warrant	Zabt
Jabin	To overcome; to overpower	Jabri
Jabir; jabun (+M) jabur	The one who render helpless	Jabir
Jablo (K)	Dumb-like	Jablo; jabal marna
Jada (+M)	More; much	Ziada
Jadhio; jadhio kal	At any time	Jadon; jad vi
Jadi	If	Yadi
Jadu (+K) (+M)	Conjuring; deceiving; enchantment ; witchcraft; magic	Jadu
Jae	Victory	Jae
Jaede	Let it go	Jande
Jaega; jaegah	Place; land;	Jagah

	farm	
Jaejug	For ever; always	Sabjug
Jaejulum	Oppression; tyranny; coercion	Zulm
Jaejulum	Coercion	Julum
Jagah (M)	Place	Jagah
Jagao	Awake	Jag
Jagao; jagarana (+M)	To be on alert; to keep awake	Jagao
Jah	An exclamation of annoyance	Jah
Jaha kaha	Here and there; anywhere	Jahan kahan; jithe
Jaha; jahae; jahaotak	Anything; whatever	Juvi
Jahaj (+M)	A ship	Jahaz
Jahal	Cor. English jail	Jail
Jahan	At any time or something else	Jahan
Jahar (K)	Muddily	
Jahar	poison	jahar
Jahir	To make known	Zahir
Jaid	Since; seeing that	Jaid ; jad
Jaigir (+M) jaegir	A rent free tenure given in return for services	Jagir

Jaitun dare	Olive tree	Zatun rukh
Jaitun	olive	jaitun
Jaj	Judge	Jaj
Jaka (K)	Place; room	Jaga; jhuga
Jakao	To forbid; to lay an embargo on	Jakao
Jakham (+M)	A wound	Zakham
Jakhir (K)	Rice boiled in sweetened milk	Khir
Jakir; jakira;	To preserver	Zakir
Jal (+M)	A net	Jal
Jal	Net	Jal
Jala	A wide expanse of water; a sea	Jala
Jalai	An iron nail	Kil
Jalao	Burn	Jalna
Jalat	To stick to; to adhere to	Jurat
Jali (M)	Blind; contract of the eye	Jala
Jalia (M)	A forgerer; a cheat	Jaali
Jaljalao (M)	To clean to brightness	Jaljalao
Jama (+M)	Amount of yearly rent; together; total	Jama (added together)
Jamabandi (K)	A rent roll of cultivators	Jamabandi
Jamao	Coagulate	Jamana
Jamedar (+M)	A head	Jamedar

	constable	
Jamin (K)	Security; bail	Zamin (who gives security)
Jamin; jamindar (+M)	To become surety	Zamin
Jamindari (K)	An estate	Zamindari
Jan janwar	A living creature	Jan janwar
Jan pahcan	An acquaintance	Jan pahcan
Jan	A witch finder	
Jan-puran (K)	Very affectionately ; dearly	Dil-o-jan; meri jan
Jana (M)	Indefinite past tense suffix	Jana
Jana suna	Well known; acquaintance	Jana suna; jana pachana
Janam (+M)	To give birth to; to be born; to originate; to spring; to appear	Janam
Janam data	Giver of life	Janam data
Janamjug (M)	Forever; always	Janamjug
Janc	To enquire	Janc (to examine)
Jande mande	Anyhow; at random	Jande mande
Janga	The foot; the leg	Janga
Jangia	Trousers; underwear	Jangia

Janie	Perhaps	Janie
Janjal	Trouble; anxiety; difficulty	Janjal
Janmal	Offspring	Janmal; jamia; aulad
Janoa-hon	Twin children	Jore
Janti	To inform; to tell; to acquaint	Janti
Janu (+M) janeu	The sacred thread worn by Hindus	Janu
Janwar (M)	Animal	Janwar
Janwar	An animal	Janwar
Jao (+M)	Barley	Jao
Jaora; jarwa	To assemble; to collect	Joria
Japri (K)	A network of bamboo places on the ridges of a roof to prevent the thachet from being blown off by the wind	Jhapri
Jar (K)	Net	Jal
Jar mar	Roots; tubers etc. dug up in the jungles for food	Jar mar (Pb. Also used for a friend's betrayal)
Jari (K) (+M)	To enforcing order	Jari
Jari buti (+M)	Medical	Jari buti

	herbs and roots	
Jarib	To measure land	Jarib
Jaribana	To impose a fine	jarmana
Jarimana (K) (+M) jurbana	Fine	Jarmana
Jarur (+M)	To require; necessary; need	Zarur
Jarur	Indispensable	Jarur
Jashulia (K)	Rice cooked in steam or hot vapors	Ubalna; jush dena (also used); jushanda is derivation
Jasu	Detective	Jasus
Jat (+M)	Caste; gender; temperament; race	Jat
Jat	Caste	Jat
Jata	A portion of the hair allowed to grow and become matted as is the habit of some ascetics and jogis	Jatan
Jatak	At once; immediately	Jatak
Jatala; jatali	A person who has allowed hisor her hair to grow long	Jatala; jatali

	and matted	
Jatan	Adhesive as clay	
Jate	In whatever way	Jewin
Jati	Temperament; nature; propensity	Jati
Jatia	Of or belonging to the caste	Jat
Jatna	As much as	Jitna
Jatra (M)	Festival; fair	Jatra; mela
Jawa	Twins	Jore; jurwan
Jawae	Husband; bridegroom	Jawae (Pb. daughter's husband)
Je; jege	Whatever; what	Jewin
Jeb	A pocket	Jeb; boja
Jehel; jehel khana (M)	Jail	Jail
Jekre	As if rooted or anchored	Jakre
Jeno	So that; in order that	Jewn
Jer; jeir (M)	Root	Jar
Jera	To cross question	Jhera
Jere jere	To be reduced; the process of reduction	Jere jere
Jerket	To copulate	Jufti
Jesan	As	Jesan
Jeth	May-June	Jeth
Jhaba	A hanging	Chat; chaba

	shelf; baskets for carrying earth slung at each end on the shoulder	
Jhabrahi	Well knit frame	Chabri
Jhae	To faint	Jhae; jhona
Jhagra	A quarrel	Jhagra
Jhagraitha; jhaagrahi; jhagrahila	Quarrelsome	Jhagralo
Jhak; Kajia	Altercation	Jhak; Kajia
Jhaka jhaki	Jostling and pushing	Pb. looking peevishly
Jhakao	To attract; to draw	Jhakao
Jhakmakao (M)	To shine; to flash	Jhakmakao
Jhakmar	perforce	Jhakmar
Jhal jhal	To glisten; to glitter	Jhal jhal
Jhalak (+M) jhalkao	Glimpse; flash	Jhalak
Jhalak malak	Decked out for shew	Jhalak malak
Jhalak	Flash	Jhalak
Jhali (+M)	A snap; trap net	jali
Jhalmal	Clean and bright	Jhalmal
Jhalui jhalue; jhalun; jhalur	To hang over or down ; baggy	Jhulna
Jham jham	To rattle as of a certain hollow	Jham jham

	ornament with small pieces of metal or stone inside	
Jhamela	Numerous; in large numbers	Jhamela (confusing too)
Jhanda; jhandi (+M)	A flag	Jhanda; jhandi
Jhanra (M)	Sieve	Chanini
Jhant (M)	Hair on the private parts	Jhant
Jhaora jhauri	To pester; to worry	Jhora
Jhaorao	To wither; to be scorched	Jhurna
Jhap (M)	To hurl oneself into	Jhap
Jhap mente	Quickly; immediately	Jhat mente
Jhapni	To cover as lid	Capni
Jhapon	To cover anything under a basket; as chickens	
Jhapta jhapti (+M) jhaptao	To snatch; to scramble for	Jhapta jhapti
Jhar	A bush; clump	Jhar
Jhar jhar	Pelting as rain	Jhar jhar
Jhar jhur	Stripped as tree of leaves	Jhar jhur
Jhar	Bush	Jhar

Jhara	Sweeping	Jhara
Jharao	To reduce; to pare	Jharao
Jhare patare	Bush and brake	Jhare patare
Jharna	A spring of water	Jharna
Jharo	To cure diseases by mantras	Jhara
Jhata	Branches fixed in the ground for climbing plants to climb up	Jhata (Pb. Fluffed and uncombed hair)
Jhatkao	To lose flesh; to be pulled down	Jhatkao
Jhatpat	Quickly	Jhatpat
Jhatpatao	To attack immediately	Jhatpatao
Jhausau	To scorch	Jhulsao
Jhemthe	To stick together	Jhurmat
Jhet; Jeth	First born; eldest	Jeth; jetha
Jhiki	To beg hard	Jhak marna
Jhile mile	Shining; polished	Jhile mile
Jhilo	To swing; a child's swing	Jhoola; peeng
Jhim jhimi	An ear ornament	Jhim jhimi
Jhiri jhiri	To trickle	Jhiri jhiri
Jhit	To irrigate	Jhata

Jhogor	To quarrel	Jhagara
Jhograhi; JHograhia	Quarrelsome	Jhagralo
Jhokao	To attract	Jhokao
Jhol	Anything hanging from the roof	Jhol; jholna
Jholnga	Reaching to the feet as garment	Jholnga
Jhompa (M)	A cluster or bunch	Thaba
Jhond; jhund	A patch of dense forest	Jhond
Jhonda	Weak through illness	Jhonda
Jhula (K) (+M) jhola	A cloth bag; a knapsack	Jhula; jhola
Jhulau	To become weak or emaciated	Jhulau
Jhumur (M)	A song sung in Tamar area	Jhumur (Pb. a group dance)
Jhund (M)	Bunch; a thick gathering	Jhund
Jhund	Herd	Jhund
Jhunka	Hollow bell-shaped ornament of bell metal; having small stone or iron pellets inside which rattle when the	Jhumka

	wearer walks	
Jhupri (+M)	A shelter made of branches	Jhupri
Jhurat; jhurao	To be over-ripe; dry through being over-ripe	Jhur jana
Jhuta mutha	Leaving of food; half eaten food; pretending; make believe	Jhutha mutha
Jhuta; Jhutha (+M)	False; liar	Jhutha
Jhutian	To seize by the hair	Jhata
Ji; jidha (M)	To be obstinate; to make a determination	Zid
Ji; jiu (M)	Life	Jewan
Jiau (+M)	To preserve alive	Jiau
Jib dan	Gift of life	
Jib jontu	Living creatures	Jia janat
Jib	Life	Jiv
Jib; jiba	Life	
Jid; jidahi; jadat; jidhi (+M)	To be persistent; preserve	Jid (stubborn)
Jid;jidhi	persevere	jid;jidhi
Jila (M)	A district; a division of	Zila

	country; an administrative unit	
Jili ladu	A kind of sweetmeat	Ladu
Jima (M)	Charge; custody	Zuma
Jin (+K)	A spirt; a ghost	Jin
Jind	To excel; to win	Jit
Jingia (K)	A bathing or short trousers	Jangia
Jinis (+K) (+M)	A thing; an article; property; goods; wealth; crops	Jinis
Jio; jia (M)	Blessing; to bless	Jeo
Jion	Life	Jion; jewan
Jira (+K)	Carraway seed	Zira
Jisu (+M)	Jesus	yasu
Jita	Life	Jita
Jitau (+M) jitao	To conquer; to win	Jitau
Jivat	Living	Jiunda
Jiwet	To become alive; living; life	Jiwet
Jiwi	Life; soul; spirit; to be patient; to yearn for	Jiwi

Ji'-la (M)	Patience	Jia
Jlaw (K)	To howl	Jhal
Jobab Dahi	Responsibility	Jowab dahi
Jobab	To reply; to answer	Jowab
Joban (+M)	Word; to promise	Zaban
Jobod (+M)	To attach property under a warrant	Zabat
Jog	To conspire; to defraud; conspiracy; collusion	Pb. Ascetic ; life style of abandoning the world; a school of thought
Jogar; jogaria	To take care of; to store carefully; to lay by	Jogar
Johok johke	Up to; equal with	Johok (Pb. Jhok; a small village)
Johok johok	Hanging; bowing; reaching far down ; as cloths on the person	Jhuk jhuk
Johot mohot	Falsely; To delay	Jhot mot
Johot; johot	Urgency; unremitting; busy	Jhat
Johrao	To collect necessaries	Jorao; jorna
Jojao	To pass life	Jojna (dealing

		with complexities of life)
Jojna	To bring up an old accusation; or a matter that has been settled	Jojna
Jok	A leech	Jok
Joka (M)	Equal; to aim	Joga (like in karan joga)
Joke	To sweep	
Jokha (+M) joka	To measure	Jokha
Jokha	Measure	Jokha
Jokhom	A wound	zakham
Jokhon	When	Jadon
Jolha (M)	Weaver	Jolaha
Jolha	Weaver	Julaha
Jolon	To be hot; inflamed	Jolon
Jolpan	Lunceon; of something that does not require cooking	Jalpan (Pb. pani wani)
Jom hudar; Jom raja (M)	One of the angles of death	Jam
Jom	Angel of Death	Jam
Jon; jona	A person	Jana
Jondra (M)	Maize	Jandra (lock)
Jonjal	Anxiety; trouble	Janjal
Jonoke	A broom	Jharo
Jonom	Birth	Janam

Jop (K)	To conquer	Jupna (to catch; to grab)
Jor (K)	The essence of elements; semen	Zor; sat
Jor (M)	Force	Zor
Jor Julum	Violence	Jor Julum
Jor bajor; jor bandhi	Forcibly	Jor bajor; zor bzor
Jor bandhao	To give heart to; take heart	Jor bandhao
Jor bhanga	To pair; to be broken by the death of one	Jor bhanga
Jor	Force	Jor
Jora (M)	A pair	Jora
Jora; jhora (M)	Caste of boatmen	Jhor
Jorao (+M)	To join; to add together; to add up; to yoke	Jorao
Jorao	Fabricate	Jorna
Jorha	Match; mate	Jorha
Joro	The areal roots of the Banyan and some other trees	Jaran
Jorwar	Strong; dominating	Zorwar
Jot	Cultivate	Jot
Jot; jotice	A pair; match; fellow	Jot
Jota	A shift (of ploughing); a	Jota. jotra

	change	
Jota;pali	shift	jota
Jotdar	The occupier of an agricultural holding	Jotdar
Jote (M) joti	The rope by which animals are yoked by the neck	Jotar
Joto	All; one and all	Joto
Ju-ula; jula; (M)	Kitchen; hearth	Chulha
Jua (+M)	Playing card; dice; gambling	Jua
Jua	Dice	Jua
Juab	Answer	Jawab
Juan	Adoloscent	Juan
Juban	Word; speech	Zaban
Juda; juda judi (+M)	Different; separate	Juda; juda judi
Judi	If	jadi
Judu	Enchantment	Jadu
Jug (+M)	Age; time; era	Jug
Jugajug; jugejud	Always; forever	Jugajug
Jugi	Ascetic	Jogi
Juh (K)	To feel quite at home	Juh (area)
Juhai (K)	A kind of sweet-scented rice	Zarda

Juhran; jurau	To collect by littles	Juran
Juk (K)	A kind of leech	Juk
Juktan	To amass; to accumulate	Joran; Jutkan
Jula (M)	A jacket	Cula (Pb. the structure to yoke the bullocks)
Julap (K)	A purgative medicine	Julab
Jule (M)	To kindle; to burn	Jalana
Julum (K)	Inconsiderately; oppressively	Zulam
Jum	Persistency	Jum
Jumla (M)	Gather; total; a collection	Jumla
Junjunau	To charge strictly	
Junom junom (K)	Forever	Janam janam
Jura (M)	To join; to stick	Jura
Juri (M)	A pair	Juri
Juri; Juridar; juri jola	A mate; a match; to mate	Juri
Juridar	Fellow	Jotidar
Jurta	To get; to obtain	Jurta
Juru (M)	To surround; to throng around	Juru
Jut (K)	False-pains	Jhut
Jut jat	To repair; to	Jut jat

	put together; to make an amicable settlement; to introduce concord ehere before there was dissension	
Jutha (M)	Leavings of one's food	Jutha
Juti (K)	Shoe	Juti
Jutic	To add; to give more to	Jutic
Jutrau	To prepare; to put to rights; to be right	Jutrau
Juwan	A youth; a maiden	Juwan
Juwari (K)	A gambler	Juwari
Jymma (K)	To collect; to sum	Jama
Jympor (K)	A jumper or lever	Jambor
Jynlat	A feast	Ziafat
	# K	
Kabalia	A cabulee; an Afghan	Kabli
Kabar	Grave	Kabar
Kabar; chitar-kabar	Spotted; specially; red and white	Chitkabra
Kabbar; khawar	Prison; imprison	

Kabea kobea; kabua	Crooked; bent	Kuba
Kabekebe; kehbekebe	Crooked; bent	Kuba; kub
Kabel; kabil (+M) kabil	Capable; skillful; expert	Kabel
Kabil	Capable	Kabil
Kabja	Hinge	Kabja
Kaboj (+M) kabja	Occupier; possession	Kaboz; kabza
Kabor; Kaburi	A grave	Kabar
Kabu	To subdue; tame; control	Kabu
Kabul (M)	To agree; to admit; to accept	Kabul
Kabuli (M)	An Afghan	Kabuli
Kabuliat (+M)	The counter-part of a lease	Kabuliat
Kac (+M)	Glass	Kac
Kac	Glass	Kach
Kaca	Raw	kaca
Kaca; kaci (+M)	Unripe; immature; raw	Kaca; kaci
Kaca; kacni; kaci	A piece of cloth worn round the loins; underwear	Kacha
Kacahri (+M)	A court-house	Kacahri
Kacal	To hamper; to impede	Kucal

Kacao; keecao	To repeatedly lift up and throw down ; as women do when washing cloths	Kacao; phandna
Kacar; kacor	Dirty; miry	Kacra
Kacauri	Sweet bread	Kacaucri
Kachahari	Court	Kachahari
Kachim	Tortoise	Kachu
Kachim; kachima; Kachmi (M) kachua	A tortoise	Kachu kuma; kachwa
Kacmacao	To be restive	Kacmacao; kasmasao
Kacokam	To forget; to overlook; to perform work inefficiently	Cok
Kad (K)	To tear; to rend	KAT
Kad	Prison; to imprison	Kad
Kada koda	To bend down	Koda
Kada	A buffalo bull	Kata
Kadal (M)	Plantain	Gha
Kadam; kadom (+M)	A step; an ambling trot taught by natives of India to their horses	Kadam; kadom
Kadar (+M)	Method; way; manner; mode;	Kadar

	custom; modus operandi ; values	
Kadha kadhi	To take a little from each	Kadha kadhi
Kadhiau	To take out some with the hand;	
Kadi	A female buffalo calf	Kati
Kadlak	A tree up till half grown	Kadlak
Kadraha; kadrahi	Quarrelsome (male and female)	Khere
Kadu (+M) Kadua	A species of pumpkin	Kadu
Kadwa; kadua; kadwi	Lame; limping owing to one legshort	Kaido (as in Heer Ranjha story)
Kaed; Kaedi (M)	Prison; prisoner	Kaed; kaedi
Kaende	More than half grown; as fruit	
Kaera	The plantain tree and fruit	Keara
Kagaj; kagat (+M)	Paper	Kagaz; kagat
Kaha (K)	Who; which	Kahda
Kaha kahi (+M)	To discuss angrily	Kaha kahi
Kahait (K)	To attempt to bite	Katan; katna

Kahan	When; where	Kahan
Kahani	saying	kahani
Kahani; kahni (+M) ka-ani	Story	Kahani
Kahao	To be called or named	Kahao (leading prayer singing)
Kahar (+M)	Palki or doli bearers	Kahar
Kahar kahur	Weeping loudly	Kahar
Kahe khatir	Why; wherefore; for what reason	Kahe khatir
Kahele (M)	Why?	Kahe-lai
Kahi	Whether	Kahi
Kahite	For what reason	Kahite
Kahtuk	Traditional lore; ancient; a proverb	Kahawat
Kahtukia	Well versed in traditional lore	
Kahu	A crow	Kan; kuwa
Kahwaiya	A great talker	
Kai (R)	Where; who; whom; that	Kai
Kaidau	To subdue; to imprison	Kaidau
Kaidi	Convict	Kaidi
Kaigodi (R)	Elsewhere; wherever	Kai-godi; kai-ja
Kaina (M)	I won't	Kai-na
Kaj	Work	Kaaj
Kajar	Black; lamp-	Kajal

	black with which eyelids are painted	
Kaje kajeto	Owing to work or business	Kaje
Kaji (M)	To speak; to say; to tell	Kehna
Kaji-kaniah (M)	Folk tales	Lok-kahani (kahan lok)
Kaji-seterni (M)	Research of the word	Akhar-sian
Kajia	To quarrel; to wrangle	Kazia
Kajibara (M)	To tell about; to spread a rumor; to publish	Kanlekha; loti lawna
Kajra; kajri	Dark grey	Kajra; kajri
Kak (R)	Uncle	Kaka
Kak	Cor. English cork	Kak
Kaka (+M)	Uncle; father's younger brother	Caca (Pb. kaka is young boy)
Kaka (R)	Baby shit	
Kaka; Mama	Uncle	Chacha;Mama
Kakh	Armpit	Kach
Kaki	Aunt; wife of father's younger brother	Chaci
Kaki;Mami	Aunt	Chachi; Mami
Kakkak	Caw caw of the crow	Kakkak

Kakla (M)	To talk; to converse; to call loudly; talkative	Kokna; kok; kukara
Kaklista (R)	Loom; spinning wheel	Katna; khadi; carkha
Kako; Kakorro (R)	Uncle; dear uncle	Kako; cacu
Kakra	A common lizard	Kirla
Kal (M)	Machine	Kala
Kal	Time	Kal
Kal bhag	Lease of life	Kal bhag
Kal kal	Numerous; very many	Kal kal
Kal katao	To spend or pass time	Kal katao
Kal	Machine	Kal
Kal; kol	Any machine	Kal
Kalak; Kalank	Suspicious; scandal; fault; reproach; accusation	Kalak; kalank
Kalapani (M)	The sea; to transport as a convict	Kalapani
Kalha	Cold	Kuhra
Kali baxt (R)	Tragic fate	Kale bakhat; bad-kismat
Kali piaj	Onions raised from bulbs	Kali piaz
Kali yug	The fourth and last period of	Kalyug

	Hindu division of historical times; the worst and polluted period	
Kali	Ink; accusation; calumny	Kali
Kali-yakh (R)	Black eye	Kali akh
Kalkal	Distressingly; gnawing sensation	Kilkil
Kalkalao (+M)	To annoy by making a din; to make a noise	Kilkalao; kilkil
Kalo (R)	Black	Kala
Kalo-kanrro	Blackthorn	Kala kanda
Kalom	Engraft	Kalam
Kalorro; kalugo (R)	African; black	Kalorro
Kalpao (M)	To suffer pain	Kalpao; kalpna
Kam jari; kami jari	To transact business	Kam jari
Kam	Work; business	Kam (Pb. sex as well)
Kamahi	To loose time	Kamahi
Kamai (+M)	Earnings	Kamai
Kamal (M)	Lotus	Kamal; kanwal
Kamani	The ribs on an umbrella	Kamani
Kamao	Earn	Kamao
Kamar	Blacksmith	Pb. Lohar; kamiar is potter
Kamari	The money	Lohara

	paid for the blacksmith's work	
Kambla; kamla	A kind of tree	Kanwal
Kambra	Blanket	Kambal
Kamda	To copulate	Pb. Kami is sex indulgent; or addicted to sex
Kami (+M)	Worker	Worker (Pb. all artisans are called kami)
Kamia (+M)	A male farm servant	
Kamia-boro (M)	Hard worker	Buhta-kami
Kamin ; kamrt	A female farm servant	
Kamini	Wife of a farm worker	Pb. general word for degradation of females. May have been derived from 'Kamini'
Kamkaj	Businees	Kamkaj
Kamlo (R)	Love; like; make love	Kam (sexual desire)
Kamra (M)	Woolen blanket	Kambal
Kamri (M)	Maid-servant	Kamri
Kan (R)	Ear	Kan
Kan jari	The part of the facein front of the ear	Kan jari
Kan phuka	To blow in the ear; suborn; to	Kan phuka

	induce false witness	
Kan	Ear	Kan
Kana (R)	When; while	Kad
Kana kona; kana kuni	The corners	Kona; banna
Kanabasi (M)	Yoke hook	Kanh (neck of bullock)
Kanas	Anger	Khunas
Kanci; Kbanchi	A basket	Khanci
Kancur	Slough of a snake	Kunj; skunj
Kanda	A waterpot of a certain size	Pb. Kunda; an earten or stone bowl to mix and crush various spices.
Kandal; Kandimos; Kandimo	Follow advice; attention; obedient	Kan dharna; kan laona (all derived from kan)
Kandalo (R)	Having large ears	Kharkana
Kandhar	A cave or hollow under an overcharging bank	Kan is kinara and dhara is wave of water
Kandi	The mortar of a dhinki in which the grain is put	Kuthi
Kandom (M)	Brink or edge of a vessel	Kandha
Kangli; khangli (R)	Comb	Kangi
Kankan	Lancinating; feeling of	Kankan

	pain	
Kankanao	Throbbing; aching;	
Kankar	quartz(gravel)	kankar
Kanki (M)	To look with one eye closed	Kanakhi
Kankotra	Earwig; secretly listening	Pb. Extremely clever
Kanla; kanlaha	Poor; destitute	Kangla
Kanphul; kanphuli	An ear ornament	Kanphul
Kanrro (R)	Thorn; stinger	Kanda
Kanta (M)	Weighing scale	Kanta
Kanta-mari (M)	Small-pox	Kali mata
Kantha	Patchwork; old cloth sewn together so as to make a whole piece without holes in it	Pb. Gudri
Kapa (M)	To throw into the mouth	Ghap karna
Kapar	Head	Kapar
Kapasara	A poetical name for raw cotton	Kpah
Kapat	One piece of a door	Kapata (ik pasa)

Kapat;Darwan	Door	Kapat;Darwaza
Kapci	Scissors	Kanci
Kapi (M)	A kind of axe	Kuhari
Kapi	A battle-axe	
Kapta kapti	To quarrel and pull or strike each other	Kapta kapti
Kapti (M)	Deceitful	Kapti (one who indulge in kapat)
Kapur (+M)	Camphor	Kaphur
Kapur	Camphor	Kapur
Kar (M)	Rent; compensation	Kar (kar kamaona; Waris Shah)
Kar (R)	Penis (used in polite conversation)	
Kara	A large iron pan used to boil sugar cane juice in	Kara (Pb. Halwa sweetmeat is also nicknamed as such)
Kara; karha (M)	Earth mover; used in leveling earth; to level the earth	Karha; karahna (levelling)
Kara; kari	Blind male and female	Pb. not used but drived from kor meaning blind
Karahi (+M)	A round flattish dish; sometimes of iron but mostly of	Karahi

	earthenware; frying pan	
Karai	To chastise; to beat; to punish by beating	Kutai
Karaili (M)	A vegetable	Karila
Karam dar; karam phul	A ceremony in which two persons of the same sex swear eternal friendship	
Karao	To make a kind of a bread which is fried in oil	Paratha
Karar (+M)	To promise; pledge oneself	Karar
Karba (+M)	A plough handle	
Karbar (+M)	To transect business	karobar
Karbari; karbario; karbaria (+M)	One who transects business and is conversant in it	Karobari
Karchu	Ladle	Karchi
Karha (+M)	An agricultural implement used to drag earth from one place to the other;	Karha

	the leveler	
Kari	Black	Kali
Karigar; karigol; (+K) Karikor (+M)	An artisan	Karigar
Karja (+M)	Debt; to incur debt	Karza
Karja	Debt	Karja
Karjia-jukutu	Proverb	Kahawat
Karkar	Dry; hard	Karkar
Karkhansa (M)	Workshop	Karkhana
Karne; karon	Cause; reason; consequential happenings	Karne
Karon	Cause	Karan
Karor karor	In multitudes; in tens of millions	Karor karor
Karor	Millions	Karor
Karra	Harsh	Karra
Karsaj; karsaji	To do work; business	Karsaz; karsazi
Karta (R)	Business; playing cards	Karta
Karya; karyo	Black	Kala
Kas (R)	Who; whom	Kas (why)
Kasa (R)	Vault; bank; pawnshop	Khesa (pocket)
Kasai (+M)	A butcher	Kasai
Kasam (+M)	An oath	Kasam
Kasao; kaskasao (+M)	To tighten	Kasao; kasso
Kasapia (R)	Butcher's shop	Kasai
Kasar	Remnant; remainder; deficiency	Kasar

Kasht (R)	Tree; lumber wood; stand for musical instrument; coffin	Kashat (cultivation)
Kashtari (R)	Woodsman; wood seller; forester	Lakar hara
Kashti;Dungi	Boat	Kashti;Dongi
Kasi	To geld; to castrate	Khasi
Kasis	Sulphate of iron	
Kaskas	Tighat	Kasas; kasia; kas
Kasmir lugri	Cashmere cloth (lungi)	Kachmir (lungi)
Kasra; khasra	The itch	Khasra
Kastao	To repent; to regret	Pachtao
Kasur (+M)	A fault	Kasur
Kat badhoe; kat badohi	A wood worker; a carpenter	
Kat	Wood	Kath
Kata (R)	From	Kithon
Kata katua; kata katwar; kata kuta	Rubbish; leaves; straws &c. which gathers about the courtyard of the house	Kura
Katao (+M)	To cut; to strike out; to live or pass time	Katao; katan

Katari (R)	Spinner; weaver	Katan wala
Kate	And or by ; in continuing a narrative	Kite
Kath (M)	Catechu; wood	Kath
Katha	Word	Kath
Kathao	Employed to introduce a statement of which the speaker has no personal knowledge	Kathao; sunisunai
Kathi (M)	Fuel	Kathi (from kath); balan
Kathi	A measure equal to two seers	Wati
Kathin	Difficult; serious; obstinate; unkind	Kathin
Kathli	A small wooden cup for holding oil	Kupi
Kathor	Cruel	Kathor
Kathor; kathoria (+M)	Cruel; merciless; relentless; obstinate	Kathor
Katik (M)	Month of Katik	Kata
Kato	A knife of a peculiar shape used	Caku

	by Mahle basket makers; a knife to pare mangoes &c.	
Katu (M)	Wooden shoe or slippers	Kharawan
Kau; Kaua (M)	Crow	Kan; kua
Kaudi	A shell used money; price	Kaudi
Kaura	Hot; pungent	Kura (bina klag)
Kawar	A door in two pieces	kawar
Ke (R)	Your	
Ke	Active verbal particle used in conditions; every; each; by	Ke
Kecha (M)	To tear into small pieces	Katarna (katran; the pieces)
Keola	A leech	Lekh
Ker	To surround; to enclose	Gher
Keraya (+M)	Rent	Keraya
Kesapo (R)	Butcher	Kasai; kasab
Keskese	Tight; stiff	Keskese
Ketab	Book	Kettab
Keti	To till; to cultivate	Kheti
Khaak	Greedy; ravenous; gluttonous; hungry	Ghagh
Khabar (M)	News	Khabar
Khabardar (M)	To be on alert	Khabardar

Khabardar	Take care; look out; to be alert	Khabardar
Khac khac	An unending verbal fighting	Khac khac
Khaca	A pice; one fourth of an anna	
Khacake	To pierce as a thorn	Khubke
Khacakhac	Shoulder to shoulder; full to the limit	Khacakhac
Khacao	To pack close; to shoulder	Khacao
Khacar	Mule	Khachar
Khacara khucra	To break into pieces	Kacra
Khachraha (M)	Wicked	Khacra
Khackhacao	To worry	Khackhacao; kicatani
Khacraha; khacrahi	Ill-natured; bad tempered; ill conditioned	Khacra; khacri (Pb. deceitful male and female)
Khad (K)	To shovel	Khatna ; khodna
Khad	A pit	Khad
Khada bhusa	Mixed with chaff	Gatawa
Khada gada	A pit from which earth has been dug	Khada gada
Khadan (M)	A quarry or mine	Khan

Khadbad	Miry; muddy; perplexed in mind	Khadbad
Khadbadao	To be perplexed in mind	Khadbadao
Khadea; khadra	Bare; stripped as a tree of leaves	Pb. khoda; who has no chin hair
Khadi	The core of corn after the grain has been stripped off	Khadi
Khai khai	A wheezing cough	Khang
Khajana (M)	Treasury; store room	Khazana
Khajanei	Treasury	Khajana
Khajanti	A treasury; a treasurer	Khazanci
Khajmanshi (K)	A treasurer	Khazanci
Khak (K)	Tightly; firmly	Kas; kasna
Khal	To flay; to skin	Khal
Khal; Khala dabha	Deep; as pool of water; deep stagnant water; distress; difficulty	Pb. Khala; a passage dug for water flow to irrigate crops
Khalah (K)	Throw up as with a shovel	Khala (narrow passage dug out for irrigation water)

Khalas (K)	To let loose; to dismiss; to get discharged	Khalas
Khalas	To set free; to acquit	Khalas
Khali (M)	Empty	Khali
Khali	Vacant	Khali
Khalis; khalsa	To be relieved of encumbrance in the stomach or intestines	Khalasi
Khalki (K)	A window	Khirki
Kham (K)	More	Kham (buhta)
Khama (M)	To forgive	Chama
Khamca khamci	To seize; to tug or pull at each other	Khicatani
Khamid; khamind	Master; head of household	Khasam; khawind
Khan ge	Then	Khan ge
Khana khaji	Not restricted to what one can eat	Khana khaji
Khana; khana pina	Food; food and drink	Khana; khana pina
Khanas khonos	To sulk	Khanas khonos
Khanca (+M)	A large basket	Khanca
Khand (R)	Smell; odor; stench; stink	Gandh
Khand;Hisa	Division	Khand;Hissa
Khanda (M)	A sword; to cut in two	Khanda (khand or khan mean parts)

Khandao	To divide; to make into divisions	Khandao
Khande khand	All; leaving out nothing; all as it occurred	Khnid phut
Khandha	A trench used as a fireplace when cooking has to be done for a large number of people	Khuddi; khandak
Khando	A break or gap in a ridge or line; a gap made by a lost tooth; a breech; notched; hacked	Khando; bora (if gap made by lost tooth)
Khanj	Notch; slit; socket	Khanc
Khanjri	A small drum beaten by fingers	Khanjri
Khanta gada	A pit from which earth has been dug out	Gada; toya
Khaowar	Foolish	Khaowar
Khap (K)	A big drain in a hali land or a dich round a dence	Khali
Khap	A notch; a	Khapa

	hollow into which another piece of wood is fixed	
Khapao (M)	To fit up a covering or lid or cork	
Khapao	To spend or pass time	Khapao
Khapra (+M)	A roofing tile	Khapra
Khapri	The skull	Khopri
Khapua		Depressed; hollow; sunken
Khar (K)	To salt the curry	Khar (khara is lona or saltish)
Khar khor	Rustling; rattling; cracking sound	Khar khor; kharak
Khara (K)	Of the same good size;	Khara
Khara khari	Decent; honorable; paying what is due; clean in transections	Khara khari
Khara	Decent	Khara
Kharai	A ditch; a trench	Khudi
Kharake	To clean the throat; phlegm; slimy matter ejected from the mouth	Khangora

Kharan	Barren; waste; desolate; as a country	Kharan (where water is khara or saline)
Kharana	Saline soil	Khari miti
Kharap	Bad; evil; wicked	Kharab
Kharapa	A kind of sandal	Kharawan (wooden slippers)
Kharas	Hard; lumpy	Kharas (Pb. A bullock pulled machine to grind flour &c. just like the one to juice the sugar cane)
Kharca (+M)	Uncooked food; money for food	Kharca
Khari mati	Chalk	Chalk
Kharij (+M)	To dismiss; or reject as a petition or complaint	Kharij
Kharkaha; kharkahi	Expert; proficient	Kharkaha
Kharku	High; tall	Pb. An overwhelming personality
Kharu patu	Restless; restive as an animal	Khowro
Kharu	An ornament worn on the ankles by women	
Khas	Itch	Khaj

Khasi (M)	Castrate; to geld	Khasi
Khasi	Casterate	Khasi
Khat khot	A written document; a letter	Khat khot
Khata khati	By groups companies or division	Khata khati
Khata	A group; a division	Khata
Khatam	Finish	Khatam
Khatao	To work; to labor; to slave	Khatao; khatna
Khatar khatar	Sound of crunching	Kharak
Khatir (M)	To be patient; consolation	Khatir
Khatir	On account of; owing to; for this reason	Khatir
Khatir; Khatir jama; khatir joma	To be comforted; to be consold; to be assured	Khatir jama
Khatkhatao	To screes like a frightened bird	Pb. to knock
Khatlak	A small bed	Khat
Khatlak; khatlao	To behead	Katal
Khatna	To circumcise	Khatna
Khatoea; khatwaia	Industrious	Khatao
Khatom	To finish; to	Khatam

	put an end to	
Khatpat; khatpatao (+M)	To be at variance; to be hostile to each other	Khatpat
Khatra		
Khatra	Dangerous	Khatarnak
Khaua; khaua khawi; khawia	An eater; a free loader	Khau
Khauk	Deep; pit	Khai; khad
Khaukha; kankha	Rim of a vessel	
Khaver/kaver (R)	Another; other; next	Keval; hor
Khaw Khaw (K)	Peniless	Khukh
Khawao	To feed; to give food to	Khawao
Khawia (K)	To reach out and pull a thing by means of a long stick	Khundi
Khaya kurca	To tear into fragments	Kucrna
Kheal	To imagine; to fancy	Kheal
Khechra (M)	Anything badly done	Khackia
Kheja	Cesses levied Zamindars on their ryots; generally in kind	
Khel	play	khel
Khelwar; khelwari; khelwaria	A performer as at dance	Khadari

Khenha; kehna; keuha	Daughters to collect prerequisites at home before marriage; to lay past	Pb. The closest word is gehna meaning jewelry
Khepao	To spend or pass time	Khepao
Kher (R)	Home; house	Ghar
Khere khore; khara khore	Uneven; unsymmetrical	Kharwa; kharwra
Khere; kherwed	Litlle; a term of endearment	
Kheroc	Chipped	Kheroc
Kherunto (R)	Domestic; domesticated; household	Gharelo
Khet	A rice field	Khet (Pb. any field)
Kheti Bari	Cultivation	Kheti Bari
Kheti; kheti bari	Cultivation	Kheti; kheti bari
Khia (K)	With a revengeful spirit	Kheh; khehna
Khiau piau	To give food and drink	Khiwao piawo
Khiau	To feed; to give food to	Khilao; khiwao
Khic khic	Suppressed laughter	Kheh kheh
Khica; kica	Unripe; immature	Kaca
Khidi khidi	To make into	Khidi khidi

	small pieces	
Khie (K)	To go away; to get up	Geie; khiskna
Khijan	To nag; to irritate	Khijan
Khijla khijli	To be irritated	Khinjia
Khijur	A common palm tree	Khijur
Khil (R)	Butter	Khir (milk)
Khil	A nail of wood	Khil
Khilap (M)	Adverse; against	Khilaph
Khilauna	Toy	Khilauna
Khilauna; khelaona	A toy	Khilauna
Khilla (M)	A nail	Kil
Khing (K)	To resist	Khungi; khung (Something that comes in the way)
Khir	Rice cooked in milk	Khir
Khirki (+M)	A window	Khirki
Khirki	Window	Khirdki
Khis; khis khisau; khaisa khaisi (+M)	To be irritated; to be annoyed	Khijna; khij
Khlei (K)	To cast out of the mouth; to spew	Kuli
Khlong (K)	To pull out of a narrow place	Khicna; khic
Khoa (M)	Condensed milk	Khoa

Khober	News	Khabar
Khobor	Information	Khabar
Khodao	To cave; as letters on a stone	Khodao
Khodna; khudni	Tatooing male and female	
Khodrao	To cut; to scrap	Kharad
Khoedak; khoedok; khaeduk	A pit; a mine	Khandak
Khoj puchar	To consult; to seek	Khoj puchar
Khoj	seek;to	khoj
Khok	To cough	Khang
Khol	Hollow	Khol
Kholao	To hollow out	Kholao
Khomokhah	In vain; without cause	Khahmukhah
Khondlak; khondlak	A pit; a gully	Khandak
Khones	Hatred; ill will	Khones
Khonja	To get bogged; to be in tight place	Khonja (Pb. extreme corner; khonje lagna is to be cornered).
Khonta	An instrument for digging holes; generally fix posts in it	Khonta (Pb. The pole with which animals are tied)
Khora	The vessel which receives the	Kaura (lately tin made pipa was used for that)

	juice of the sugar cane when being pressed	
Khorag; khorak	Food; an advance of wages for food	Khorak
Khoraki	An advance of pay	Khoraki
Khorana	Saline	Khara (as water)
Khorca; kharca	Food; rice; to spend	Kharca
Khot	Tarnish	Khot
Khota; khotao	To rake up old stories; to blame; to accuse	Khota (Pb. impure; deceitful; one who can betray)
Khotrao; khodrao	To scrap; to cut by scraping action	Khotarna (as of grass)
Khowao; khuao	To cause to lose; to lose	Gawao
Khub (+M)	Good; well; excellent	Khub
Khub	Excellent	Khub
Khuci	A stick with a sharp point used to make holes; a dibble	Khuci
Khucra (+M)	To break into pieces; to change as momey; small pieces	Khura; bhan

	of money	
Khucri	Turn into shreds	Khucri
Khud (K)	To scrape off	Khurcna; khudna
Khud	self	khud
Khuda khudai	Chasing; pursuing	Khuda khudai (Pb. to search deeply)
Khuili	A small pin on which cotton is rolled previous to spinning	Walna?
Khukhi; kukhi	The womb	Kukh
Khula khuli	Frankly; openly; freely	Khula khuli
Khula	Open; frank	Khula
Khula;khulasa	open	khulla;khulasa
Khulasa	Sincerity; candour; frankness;	Khulasa (summary as well)
Khulau	To narrate fully; to tell all	Khulau
Khulsasa;Rihai	Freedom	Khalasi;Rihai
Khum (K)	To fasten; to tie; to bind	Khum (khum thapna)
Khun (K)	To drag a thing to oneself	Khuhna; khicna
Khun	Blood	Khoon
Khunes	Hatred; ill will	Khunes
Khuniahi	Murderous; guilty of murder	Khuni

Khuntau	To tie or bind to a post	Khuntau
Khunti	A post	Khunti
Khupa	Hollow as opposed to straight	Kupa
Khur (K)	To scrap	Khur; khurcan
Khur (R)	Heel	Khur (animal hoof)
Khura	To search	Khura
Khura; khure	A hoof	Khur
Khura; kurha	Rinderpest	Monkhur (animal disease)
Khuri (R)	Energetic; frisky young woman	Kuri
Khurpa; khurpi	An instrument for digging or scrapping	Khurpa; khurpi
Khusi; kusi (+M)	To be pleased; to be satisfied; to rejoice; pleasure	Khuchi
Khuti (K)	A short post; a peg; to play draughts	Khunti
Khuti	Loss or damage	Khuti (Pb. also a small round shaped pit which is used for playing goli and banta)
Ki	Or; whether	Ki
Kian (K)	A charm; a	Gian

	magic; keenness of intellect	
Kiar (K)	To spread over; to extend	Kirna
Kicho (R)	Hip	Kuchar
Kichu bichu	Some; little	Kujh; kuch
Kickic	To be annoyed	Kic kic
Kidel (R)	Arrest; pick up; assemble; collect; gather; pick; reap; crush; press; squash; squeeze	Kidel (kaid)
Kiei (K)	Who? What	Kiei
Kijor; kjuh (K)	To cox; cajole	Kalava (lena)
Kil (K)	A vakil; a pleader	Vakil
Kila (M)	Fort	Kila
Kilau	To strike with fists on the nap of the neck	
Kilo (R)	Peg; tent peg; post	Killa
Kilodori (R)	Rope of a pole	Killa-rasi
King (K)	A wasp; a hornet	King
Kino (K)	Which	Kino
Kino kino	Any	Kino kino
Kiria (M)	Oath; to	Kilia (to make

	swear	witches and other creatures to remain within a boundary)
Kirsand	Cultivator	Kirsan
Kisand (+M) kisanr	A cultivator; a master; an employer	Kisan
Kishti	A boat	Kishti
Kisi (R)	Inside pocket in the waist	Khisi
Kisim (+M) kisism	Kind; sort; variety	Kisim
Kisim	Variety	Kisim
Kismis (K)	A raisin	Kichmich; mewa; sogi
Kismot (K)	Fate; luck	Kismat
Kist; kisti (+M) kista	An installment	Kist
Kitra kutra	To divide or make into piees	Kita kutra
Klat (K)	A glass; a tumbler	Glass
Klavo (R)	Captive; slave	Klava (To take in full embrace)
Kobe	When	Kab
Koca; konac (+M)	A corner	Koca; kona
Kodka (R)	There; right there	Kadoka
Kodo	To stoop; stooping	Koda
Kodom; kadam	A step	Kadam
Kodrao	To scrap	Khotarna
Kohna	Versed in traditional	Kohna (from Kahani; kahna;

	lore	kuna)
Koid (K)	To confine	Kaid
Koidi (K)	A prisoner	Kaidi
Koila (M)	Charcoal; coal	Koila
Koina	A virgin	Kanwari
Kokala (R)	Bones; Skelton; farming; standard	Khokha `
Kokhrao	Hollow; as an old tree	Khokhla
Kol	A machine; any mechanical contrivance	Kala
Koliba; kolibista (R)	Hut	Kuli
Kolkand	The corner rafters of a pavilion roof	Kaule
Kolom (K)	To plant a twig in the ground to grow	Kalam (lana)
Kolom	A pen; a cutting; to prune	Kalam (Pb. just for pen. In Urdu kalam means cutting &c.)
Kom; Komti	To become less; to be deficient	Kam; ghat
Komjor	Weak	Kamzor
Komora (R)	Room; chamber; hall	Kamra
Kon (R)	Who; whoever	Kon

Kona (M)	Corner	Kona
Kona	Corner	Kona
Kona; konac; konaj; konat	A corner	Kona
Konho	Anythin; anyone	Kohno
Konthekan	Who can say; who knows	
Kop	The cover; the cuff	khopa
Kopot	Insincere; tricky; deceitful; hypocritical	Kopot (Pb. opposite of pot meaning son).
Kora (M)	Husband	Kora
Kora	A boy or a young man	Kora (Pb. munda)
Korat; korot	Cor. English; court	Kort
Korbar	Business; concern	Karobar
Kordhoc	Blind	Kora; anha
Kordit (K)	Wee; calamity	Kudrat
Korec	Blunted	Khunda
Koro koro	Stooping when carrying a heavy weight	Koda koda
Korok	To attach property under a warrant	Kurki
Koroneri (R)	Corner	Kona
Korravel (R)	Blind; dazzle; make blind;	Korovel

	misinform; lose one's sight	
Korrdor	Valuable	Qadar
Korro (R)	Blind; ignorant	Kor
Kortal	Cymbal	Kartal
Korung (R)	Crow	Kan
Kos (+M)	Two miles	Kos
Koskos (+M)	Tight; tighten up	Kasia; kas ke
Kosot (+M)	To sulk; to gloom	Ksuta (not completely well)
Kot (K)	A paper; a book; a yard; to reach	Kot; kagaz
Kot sada (K)	A blank paper	Sada kagaz
Kot-shosia	A blotting paper	Siahi chus
Kotec	To break by striking with something; stone or hammer	Kutna
Kotha (+M)	An upper story ; ceiling of a room	Kotha (Pb. any room for dwelling)
Kothar (R)	Thence; from there	Kothar
Kothi (M)	A bank; a business house	Kothi (any big house)
Kotkudi (K)	A paper kite	Gudi (Ko is paper and kudi is guddi)
Kotora (R)	Bits and pieces;	Kutra 1

	debris; fragments; remains	
Kput (K)	Revenge; vengeance	Kupat
Krei (K)	To scatter	Kera (from kerna)
Kren (K)	To speak	kehan
Kren-khutia (K)	To speak about unnecessary or trifling things	Khutia (time khota karna)
Kren-likhit (K)	To dwell on useless things	Likhit (nikhit)
Kren-satia (K)	To vex; to annoy	Satia (annoyed)
Kshot (K)	To squeeze; to press	Kasna
Kuar; kuara; kuari (+M)	Unmarried	Kuar; kuara; kuari
Kuba	Bent	Kuba
Kubi (+M) kobi	Cabbage	Ghobi
Kubi (M)	To bend	Kubi; kuba
Kubra	Crooked; bent	Kubra; kuba
Kuchi (R)	Cup; small cup	Kuji
Kucla	A species of eel	Kucla
Kucur kucur	Crunching sound; as when eating carrot	Kcur kcur
Kuda (M)	To roll up; to ben downward	Kuda
Kudi	A large hoe;	Kudali

	the digging implement	
Kudim (K)	Very ancient	Kadim
Kudom (K)	To gallop; trot	Kudom
Kuduru (M)	To hop on the ground	Kudna
Kuhas	Mist; haze	Kuhra
Kuhas; kuhasi (M)	Fog	Kuhar; kuhra
Kuhra	Mist	Kohra
Kuhrao	To groan; to moan	Kuhrao; kuram
Kui (R)	Elbow	Kohni
Kuila	Coal	Kola
Kuku	The cooing of a dove	Kuku
Kular (K)	To promise	Karar
Kulbut (K)	An arched wooden frame used for supporting a masonry work in an arch	Kulbut (Shoemakers also use it to widen the shoe)
Kulhi	The village street	Gali
Kuli	Cooly	Kuli
Kuluh (+M) culhu	An oil press	Kuluh
Kumbar (M)	The potter	Kumhar
Kumblau	To wilt	Kumblao; kumlaona
Kumi bisi	More or less	Ghat wadh
Kundi	Rim; as of butterfly net	Kundi
Kunji (+M)	A key	Kunji

Kup (K)	A suit of cloths	Kapra
Kupa	A skin vessel for holding oil	Kupa
Kupi	A bottle like earthenware for holding oil	Kupi
Kur (M)	Hoof	Khur
Kurau	A method of cultivation in which the forest is cut down and burnt after which seed is sown without ploughing	
Kurel (R)	Sexual intercourse	Related to kam plus kus (female organ) seems to be derivation
Kuri (+M) kuri hon	A girl	Kuri
Kuri	Female	Kuri
Kuria	A small hut	Kuthia
Kursi (M)	A chair	Kursi
Kurta (+M)	A jacket; a coat	Curta (PB. any long shirt)
Kurta	Coat	Kurta
Kurud	Anger; envy; hate; enormity	Kurud
Kurup (K)	To confiscate; to rob	Khuhan
Kurva (R)	Professional prostitute; call girl	Kanjri

Kurvari (R)	Pimp; whoremaster	Kanjar
Kusal	Pleasure; choice; favorable	Kusal; khushal
Kusta	Refuse after threshing leguminous crops	Kushta (Desi medicants burn different things in a small pot; the refuse is kushta)
Kusti (+M)	Wrestling	Kuschti
Kutam; kutasi (+M)	A hammer	Hathora
Kutet	Quarrelsome; disputatious	Kutet
Kutha	Ankle	Gitta
Kuthi (M)	Womb	Kukh; kus
Kuthi	A receptable in which rice is stored	Kuthi (Pb. any gran can be stored)
Kuthri	An apartment	Kuthri
Kuti	To cut into small pieces	Kuti
Kutkutau	To stick up or out	Kukutari
Kutna; kutni (+M)	A pimp; a pander; low; mean; base	Kutna; kutni (like in phaphekutni)
Kutra	To make into pieces	Kutra
Kutru	A dog	Kuta
Kyllep (K)	Lonely place	Akal
Kyllum (K)	In a lumpsum; whole	Kul
Kyndad (K)	A mole	Khota

Kyndong (K)	A corner	Kona; nukar
Kyndur (K)	An oven; a stove	Tandur
Kynjah (K)	Lonely	Kunj
Kynphat (K)	Cotton	Kapah
Kyrhuh (K)	To roar	Karahna; kokna
Kyrkait (K)	To shout exultingly	Kukar; kukara
	L	
Lab; labha; (+M)	Profit; greed	Lab
Labejan	At the edge of dying	Labejan
Labhao	Entice	Labh
Lablab (M)	Quickly (speaking)	Labalab
Lacan; locan	Greedy; hankering after	Lacan
Lacar (+M)	To be helpless; to be without resources	Lacar
Lacar lacar	Talkative; always chattering	Lucar lucar
Lachan	Bad habit; bad behavior	Lachan
Lachlacha (M)	Shameless	Nalaj
Lachmi (+M)	Cattle; live stock; wealth; fortune	Lachmi (Pb. mal)
Lada (M)	Over and above	Lada
Ladavel (R)	Load; pack	Ladna

Ladu (+M)	A kind of sweetmeat	Ladu
Lag (+M)	Il feeling; disagreement; quarrel	Lag (Pb. The money exchanged between wedding couples family and given to artisans who arrange things for wedding
Lag	To be due; liability; obligation to pay	Lag
Laga (M)	To become weak; to look tired	Lagar
Lagae	Including; along with	Lagae
Lagajana (M)	To become weak on account of illness	Lagajana
Lagan; lagao	To apply; fix; come in contact with; to join; to occupy; to suit; to begin; to happen; busy; to quarrel	Lagan; lagao
Lagao (M)	To join; to attach	Lagao
Lagau (M)	To aarange; to put on; to	Lagau

	fix	
Lage; lae (M)	Asking one to begin	Lago; lae (to have them start)
Lagle (+M) lagalagi	Within a short interval; of time and space	Lagle
Lagna	Investment; as money or grain on interest	Lagna
Lagti	Liability; obligation to pay	Lagti
Lah (K)	Can; able; succeed	Lah (laha is fruit of labor or interest on money)
Lah (M)	Peel off; to cut off surface	Lah
Laha (K)	Lac; sealing wax	Lai; laity
Laha	Before; in front	Laha (Pb. interest on money)
Lahanga (M)	A short loin cloth	Langot
Lahanga; lahangi	Tall	Lama; lami
Lahas	A corpse; dead body	Lach
Lai	To acquaint; to say; to repeat; to inform	Lai (Pb. fall in deep love)
Laj; laja luka	Shame	Laj

Lajao (+M)	To be ashamed; disgrace or humiliation	Lajao
Lajbij	To be ashamed; to feel disrespected	Lajbij
Lajkhauka; lajkhauki	Shameless (male and female)	Lajkhauka; lajkhauki
Lakat thakar	Tired; fatigued	Thakia; thakna
Lakelak	Hundreds of thousands	Lakhan
Lakhao (+M)	To be apparent; to be visible or known	Lakhao; wakhao
Lakhi; lukhi	Lucky (male and female)	Lakhi (Pb. to be black as well)
Lakir	Habit; to be efficient; to master; to shew aptitude for anything	Lakir (a line as well)
Lal	A kind of precious stone	Lal
Lala	A sub-caste of Hindus	Lala
Lalca; Lalci (+M)	Greedy	Lalca; lalci
Lalhar (M)	Fool; rash	Lallo
Lalkar (+M) lalkao	To coax; to wheedle; to cajole	Lalkar (Pb. to challenge)

Lalot (K) (+M) laloc	Greedy; gluttonous; selfish	Lalac
Laman	Long	Laman
Lamari (R)	West	Lama
Lamka	Tall	Lamma
Lamka; lamki	Tall and thin (male and female)	Lama; lami
Lampa (M)	Horizantal	Lama; lame rukh
Lanban; landband; lonbon; londbond	To act as a money lender or grain lender; to trade	Labana
Landha	Stubble; poor	Landha
Landi (M)	Buttock	Pb. lundi is used for having no back
Landur	To hang down; to bend over	Landur; lamkna
Lang (R)	Lame; limp	Lang
Langa (+M) langra	To be tired; to be fatigued; to be worn out as an old person	Langa (Pb. lame)
Langal (R)	Become lame	Langana
Langalo (R)	Exhibiting a limp	
Langardyol (R)	Be lamed; made lame	
Langat (M)	Naked; penniless;	Nanga

	poor	
Langimos	Lameness	
Lango (R)	Lame	Langa
Langyarel (R)	Cripple; lame	
Lanka (M)	Very far away; beyond the sea	Lanka
Lap; laplap (+M)	To catch with both hands;	Lap; laplap
Lape (K)	To plaster	Lipna; lap
Lapha	Profit	Munapha (Pb. laha)
Laphan	High; long ; to prolong	Laphan (Pb. to bragging)
Laphap	Envelope	Laphapha
Lapkao (M)	To jump on to reach something	Lapkao; lapkna
Lapra; lapri	Having hanging ears; as a dog or goat (male and female	Lapra; lapri
Lapta lapti (+M)	Rolling or tumbling over each other over the ground	Lapta; lapti
Laptao (+M)	To drag one in; to become accomplice	Laptao
Lar (M)	Saliva; a string of beads	Lari (Pb. laran wagna)
Laraka (M)	Prone to	Laraka

	fighting	
Larao	To shake; to move; to exert oneself	Larao (Pb. To instigate others to fight)
Larhai (+M) larai	To fight; to quarrel	Larai
Larhai	War	Larhai
Larka parka	Children and other belongings	Larka parka
Larkao	To fall behind	Lurkna
Larkharao	To stammer; as one very much afraid when speaking	Larkharao
Larun	To dangle; to hang loosely	Lat; latkak; latakna
Lasa (M); laslasa	Gum; sticky	Laslasa (PB. like in lasura fruit)
Lasak pasak	Sticky; uncomfortabl e feeling of the skin; mainly in the hot weather; over cooked or over ripe	Lasak pasak
Lascar; lasker (+M)	Numerous; in crowds; army	Lachkar
Lasho (R)	Excellent; good; perfect	Lash pash
Laskar	Army	Lashkar
Laslasa	Occupying much space; spread out	Laslasa (Pb. sticky)

Lasra; lasri	Talkative; garrulous; loquacious (male and female)	Lutra; luri
Lat ghat	To intermix	Lat ghat
Lat	Cor. English lord	Lord
Lata	To be attached to; cling; cleave	Lata (Pb. lati derived from lata)
Latai (M)	A thread winder	Latai
Latak; latok	Hindrance; intervention	Latak;
Latar (+M)	Under; underneath; below; to put under	Latar
Latha	To stick; to be attached to	Latha (Pb. came down; descended)
Lathea	Lazy; slow	Lathea
Lati	A skein	Lati
Latkao	To stick; to adhere	Latkao (Pb. hanging something)
Latkum	Protuberant; rising above the surrounding ground	Latkum
Latpat; latpatao	To roll; or toss about; to wallow	Latpat
Latum	To fold; a fold	Latum (to end)

Laua lagta	Quarrel; ill feeling; dispute	Pb. lagna; to clash
Lauka (+M)	A boat; a dinghy	Lauka
Laundi	Concubine	Laundi
Lautau (+M)	To return; to turn back	Lautau
Lawan	To dangle; to jerk up and down; to spring up and down;	Lawan (Pb. to have female animals mated; it can be taken as cooked food with spicies)
Lawao	To share; to divide	Lawao (Pb. to have animal mated; to have something fixed like hand pump &c.)
Lazhal (R)	Be ashamed; be embarrassed	Laj
Lazhano (R)	Shy; shy person	Laja
Lazhav	Disgrace	Nalaj
Led (+M)	Excrement of horses elephants; asses &c.	Led; lid
Ledha; lidhi	Lame (male and female)	Langa; langi
Ledhak	To be lame	Lang
Ledhod	Tall; high	Lambo
Leg; ligi	A payment or prerequisite	Neg

	allowed or sanctioned by custom	
Lehe lehe	To break up and pulverize by a plough	Lehe lehe (Pb. leh also means track made by cart and other wheeled vehicles)
Lehse (K)	To have dirty habits	Lachan
Leit-bhih (K)	To go and beg	Bhikari; bhikmanga
Lejhraha; lejhor (M)	Immodest	Nalaj (laj lahia)
Lek	Capable; fit; worthy; flirting; becoming	Lek (Pb. Lek lana means dishonoring; defaming &c.)
Lekan	Like; such	Lekan (to copy)
Lekha (+M) leka	To account; to number	Lekha
Lekhta	To quarrel; to dispute	
Lel; lino; lilo (R)	Catch; choose; accept; acquire	Lena
Lel; nel (M)	To see	Lel; nel
Lembo (+M) lembu	A lemon	Ninbo; lemon
Lembo	Lemon	Nimboo
Len	To press; to express	Len (to take)
Lenca; lenci	Lame (male; female)	Langa; langi
Lenda	Small; young; the youngest	Ladla

	of a family	
Lengra; lingri	Left handed (male; female)	Khaba; khabi
Lenjer (M)	Weak	Laghar
Leora; lar; leothe (+M) lanr	Male organ	Lora
Lep	To apply ointment; an a medicine	Lep
Ler; les	Semen	les
Lerha (M)	Lame; defective	Lula
Lerka	A child	Lerka
Leser leser (+M)	Talkative; fluent in speech	Lut lutra
Letha; lotha	To include; to implicate	Laina, laona
Letkom	To stick to; to adhere	Latkom; (latkaindra used by Waris Shah)
Lewa	Soft; pliant	Lawa (fresh and young; as a plant; human and animals)
Liblibia (M)	Soft	Libliba
Libri; libra	Greedy (female; male)	Libri; llbra
Lic	The entrails	
Lie; lei	Paste	Lei
Lija (M)	Cloth	Lira
Likha	Writing	Likhna
Likhwantia	Counting; estimating ;	

	as to how much work he should do	
Lil	Indigo	Lil;Nil
Lil; nil (+M)	Blue; the indigo plant	Nil
Lila (+M) lila nila	Entertainment; show	Lela
Lilaj (M)	Immodest; shameless	Nalaj; lalaj
Lilam (+K) (+M)	An auction	Lilam; nilam
Lilhi; lilha	Foolish; ignorant	Lilhi; lilha
Lilkan	To wheedle; to cause to long for; coax; covet; desire	Likan (from lilkna or wilkna; to yearn for)
Lipa (M)	False	Lipa (like lipa poti)
Lipat lapat	Lagging behind	
Lisi; lisind; susi	Opportunity; chance; excuse; pretense	Laisi
Lisita (R)	Fox	Lomar
Lit; nit	Now	Nit
Litir pitir	Weak; feeble	Litir pitir
Lkhit (K)	Small; useless	Nkhid
Lo (+M)	Burn; to scald	Lo (Pb. light)
Lo bir	The burnt jungle	Lo bar
Lob; lob laloc (+M)	To covet; covetousness	Lob lalac
Lobab; Nobab	A great man;	Nowab

	a prince	
Loban	Frankincense	Loban
Lobdhao (+M) lobhao	To attract; charm; allure	Lobhao
Lobhi (+M)	Greedy	Lobhi
Lochon; lachan (M)	Behavior; character	Lachan
Locor	Unnatural craving for any delicacy	Loce (from locna)
Locra; lucri	Greedy; given to stealing eatables.	Locra; lucri
Lode (+M) ladi	To load; to put one thing on another	Lada; ladan
Lodhra		A sapling; Sapling about the thickness of a man's arm
Loe (M)	The male organ of generation	Luli
Loghbhog	Near; about; almost	Lagbhag
Loha luti (+M)	Iron utensils and implements	Loha luti
Lohar	Blacksmith	Lohar
Lohok	Parabolic; proverbial	Lohok; lok
Lok (K)	A friend; husband and wife	
Loksan; Noksan; nuksan	To destroy; to injure; to	Nuksan

	perish; to die; injury; scathe; damage; havoc	
Lolopoto (M)	To pacify	Lolopoto
Lombor; Nombor; Nomor	Cor. English number	Nambar
Lond; lon (R)	Salt	Lon
Londalo; londo (R)	Salty; seasoned	Lona; khara
Londo pai (R)	Salt water; sea water	Lona pani
Longra; lungri	Unchaste; wanton; licentious; incontinent; impure	Luca; luci
Lor	Sense; ability; skill	
Lora	Necessity	Lor
Loro	To have sexual intercourse	From lora
Losh (R)	Gladness; joy	Losh (loshe laina)
Loshal; Losharel; loshyol (R)	To be joyful; cheer up	Loshe lena
Lot (+M)	A government currency	Note
Lot	A clew; part or whole of stolen property	Lut
Lota (+M)	A brass vessel used for	Lota (Pb. used for wahing body

	drinking	parts)
Lotao (M)	To return back	Lotao; moro
Lotho	Not obeying at once; required to be repeatedly told or urged	Lontha
Loug; laig (M)	To be on bad term	Lagna
Luban	Incense	Luban
Lubhau	To amuse; charming	Lubhau
Lubni (R)	Prostitute; slut; whore	
Luca	Immoral	Lucha
Luca; luci (+M)	Scoundrelly; rascally; immoral (male and female)	Luch; luci
Luca;Luci	Unprincipled	Lucha;Luchi
Lucho (R)	Kindling; tinder	Lusna
Luga; lugri (+M)	Cloth; clothing	Luga; lugri
Luhi; luhia	A small shallow iron pan	Luhi; luhia
Luhui	Iron	Loha
Luka chapa	Secrete; to do secretly	Luka chapa
Luku jono	A broom made of grass	Baukar
Lulu bachu	To coax	Lulu paco
Lum (K)	To gather; to	Lumna

	collect	
Lungu (R)	Long; extended	Lama; lami
Lur (M)	Sense; skill; ability	Lur; (Pb. under some intoxication)
Lura luri	Snatching or grabbing by several people	Lura luri
Lusar pusur	To whisper	Lusar pusur
Lut (+M)	To pillage; to rob; to plunder	Lut
Lut-phut (K)	Squandering	Lutput
Luta luti (+M)	Struggling to grab	Luta luti
Lute (K)	To spoil; to plunder	Lutan
Lutera (M)	Robber	Lutera
Luti (M)	Hank of thread	Ati
Lutia	Given to pillage; plundering; or robbing	Lutera; luto
	M	
Ma (R)	Me; myself	Main
Maamla (M)	Suit; case	Mamla
Maashkaral (R)	In the middle; from the center	Manjhdar
Macalka	Personal recognizance	Macalka (legal and trade term)
Macan	A raised	Macan

	platform or scaffold	
Macha	Approximately;	Mithia
Machrenka	Fisherman	Machera
Maci andhar	Night fall	Andhar; rat
Mackao	To be sprained; cracked; twisted	Mackao; moc
Mad (K)	To taste	Maza
Madan (K)	A plain	Medan
Madhe; modhe (+M)	From among; among; middle; center	Majh; manjh
Madoli; mandoli	A receptacle in which a charm is enclosed and worn round the neck; the upper arm or the waist.	Madoli; mandolin; tweet; taweez
Mae musi	Mother's sister or mother-in-law's sister	Masi
Magdur	Power; strength	Magdur (Pb. A wooden round piece like drums is lifted to test strength)
Magni; mangni	Without payment; graits for the asking	Mangni

Maha bhag	Great good fortune	Maha bhag
Maha	A day	
Mahadeb; Mahadeo (+M)	The Hindu deity	Mahadeo
Mahajan; mohajan (+M)	Money lender; a great man	Mohajan
Mahajon (K)	Merchant; a trader	Mahajan
Mahak (M)	Smell; odor	Mahak
Mahak	Fragrant	Mahak
Mahakal	A time of greatest distress; danger and anxiety	Mahakal
Mahal; mahala (+M) (+R)	Street; a big house; district; department	Mahal; mahala
Mahal; mohal	A huge house; a palace	Mahal
Mahara (M)	One who tends cattle	
Maharaj	Emperor	Maharaja
Maharog; mahrog	Dear; high priced; scarce	Mehnga
Mahel; mahela	Jurisdiction	Mahel
Mahima; mohima	Glory; to glorify	Mahima
Mahina; mohna	A month	Mahina
Mahina;Mas	Month	Mahina;Mah
Mahir (+M)	Gentle; patient; quite	Mahar (affection)

Mahit (M)	Neat; handsome	Mohat; mohna
Mahjud; muhjud; mahjut; mahjut (+M)	To be ready; prepared; eady at hand	Maujud (extant)
Mahla	A story	Mahla
Mahsul	Toll	Mahsul
Mahsul; masul (+M)	Rent; fare; freight; postage; toll	Mahsul; masul
Mahut (K)	Elephant driver	Mahawat
Mai	Addressing a younger female	Mai (addressing an older female)
Maia (K)	Mystery	Maia
Maila	Dirty; filthy	Maila
Mairi	A term of endearment used for female friend	Mairi
Maj; manj	Hard heart-wood ; center wood of some kinds of trees.	Maj; manj (center of anything)
Maja (M)	Pleasure	Maza
Majao;ragado	scour;to	manjo;ragado
Majbut; majgut	Strong; substantial	Mazbut
Maji (K)	Sailor	Majhi; malah
Majlis	Conference	Majlis
Majrad; majrat	To entertain; to shew respect to by hospitality	Madarat

Majur; majurii (+M)	A daily laborer; daily wage	Mazdur; mazduri
Mak; man	To slash; chop or hew with any cutting instrument as a sword; axe &c.	Kat
Makai (M)	Maize	Makai (jawar)
Makardama (M)	Suit; case	Mukadma
Makh (R)	Fly; house fly	Makhi
Makhan; makhon (+M) makhan	Ointment; to apply ointment; butter	Makhan (butter)
Makhel (R)	Grease; lubricate; oil	Makhan
Mal	Athlet	Mall
Mal; maljal (+M)	Goods; effects; merchandise	Mal (the wealth in form of cattle)
Mala (+M)	A necklace; anything of the nature of an ornament worn round a neck	Mala
Mala	Necklace	Mala
Malai (K)	Cream	Malai
Malan; malao (+M)	To rub the body or limbs; massage	Malan; malich
Maldar (M)	Wealthy	Maldar

Malgujari (+M)	Rent (of land)	Malguzari
Mali (+K) (+M)	A Gardner	Mali
Mali mambla; mali mamla	A law suit relating to finances	Mali mamla
Malik (+M)	Master; owner; lord	Malik
Malkathi	An upright with a slit in it through which the driving band (maal) of spinning wheel passes from the driving wheel to the spinning axle (taku)	Maal
Malmal; malmalia	Fine; thin cloth	Malmal
Malumala	Roughly; not properly; with force	Malumal
Mama (+K) (+M)	Maternal uncle	Mama
Mama bhagna (+M)	Uncle and nephew	Mama bhanja
Mamasi; Mamasi bochako	Cousins the female side; the relationship between children of sisters	Masair
Mami (+M)	Aunt; wife of	Mami

	maternal uncle	
Mamkur	Relatives of the mother's side with whom marriage is not allowed in Hindusism	Nanke
Man (+M)	Respect; honor; to entertain; to honor	Man; maan
Man (+M) mon	A weight of 40 seers	Man
Man (M)	A mound	Man
Man (R)	Me; myself	Main
Man marjat	To treat hospitably; to treat with distinction	Man maniada
Man	Manna	Man
Man-man (K)	Obstinately	Man-man; man-mani
Mana (+K)	To forbid; to warn; to admonish	Mana
Manadi	To proclaim; to preach; proclamation	Manadi
Manahi	Forbidden; unlawful	Manahi
Manan	Honor	Maan
Manao	To pay respect to; to honor; to	Manao

	obey	
Manda (M)	Cold; coryza	Zukam (manda is to be in bad condition)
Mandar	The head-man of the village	Mandar (Hindu temple)
Mandari	A drummer; drum musician	Mandri (specialist in curing snake bites)
Mander	N a long time; or wide circle; a wide area; a multitude	
Mandha; mandhwa; mandwa (+M)	A temporary shed or booth erected on the occasion of a marriage	Mandwa; mandap
Mandi (+M)	Cooked rice; food	Manda (Pb. like used in halwa manda
Mandil; mondil; mundil; Mandir; mondir; mudir (+M)	A temple	Mandir
Mandir	Temple	Mandar
Mandli (M)	Congregation	Mandli
Mane (+M) mano	Meaning	Mane
Mane (K)	To worship; to submit	Mane; manta
Mang (K)	To give just enough of everything	Mang (Pb. engaged; Urdu; demand)

Mangal; kusal mangal (M)	Welfare	Mangal
Mangal; mongol (+M) mangar	Tuesday	Mangal
Mangao (+M)	To send for to acknowledge	Mangao (to send to fetch something)
Mangar	An alligator	Magarmach
Mangel (R)	Ask; want; wish for	Mangna
Mangelas	Female beggar	Mangti
Mangimata (R)	Alms; proceeds in goods or money from begging	Mangan, bhekh
Mangimos (R)	Claim; demand; request; want	Mang; talab
Mani	A kind of precious stone	Mani (Mani means bread in Sindhi)
Manik (+K)	A kind of a gem said to be found in the heads of certain snakes; a pearl	Manik
Manj; manja (M)	Center wood	Pb. manja is bog cot and manji small
Manjan	Breakfast; mid-day meal	
Manjhi	A village	Malik, mahar

	chief; a village head	
Manjil (M)	A day's journey	Manzil
Manjla; manjli	The middle or an average	Manjla; manjli
Manjur (+M)	To approve of; to accept; to admit	Manzur
Manki (M)	Name of the ancient headman of a â€˜parha'	Manki
Mannite	For the asking; gratis	Mannat (from a spiritual person or deity)
Manot; manotan; manotia	Respectable; honorable	Manot
Manoti manwa (+M) manoa	Human beings	Banda
Manrna (M)	Dead body	Murda
Manrro (R)	Bread; loaf of bread	Mani (common use in Sindhi)
Mansi	Each person	Mansi
Manta	To soften; to reconcile; to persuade; to put off	Manta
Mantar	Incantation	Mantar
Mantri	Minister	Mantri
Manus man	To become well-to-do	
Manush (R)	Male human being	Manush
Manushni (R)	Female human being	Manushni

Manwa	A human being	Munwa
Map (+M) nap	To measure	Map
Map; maph (+K) (+M)maphi	To forgive	Maph; maphi
Maph	Forgive	Maph
Maphik; mapit	Like; resembling	Maphik
Maphot (K)	Free; for nothing	Muphat
Mapik (K)	Moderate; middling	Maphik (suited with)
Mar mar(K)	At once; without losing time	Maromar
Mar marmar (+M)	Quickly; instantly	Maromar
Mar muhim	Distress; suffering; affliction	Mar muhim
Mar	To finish; to complete	Mar
Mara	On the point of; about to	Mara; mare
Marak (+M) mara	A peacock	Mor
Maramat (+M)	To repair; to med	Maramat
Marao	Annihilate	Marna
Marca marci		
Mardao	To message	Malich (Pb. Mardao means manhood; bravery)
Mardo (R)	Beaten; beaten up; roughed up	Mar khada

Mardyol (R)	Be assaulted; get beaten	Mar khana
Marel (R)	Beat; hit; clobber; punch; slug; strike	Mar
Marghati; masna; masanrua	A burial place or burning place	Marghat; masan; gustan
Mari (M)	Old; aged	Pb. weak due to bad health
Mari mari (M)	Slowly	Mere mere ; masan
Mari	A corpse; a dead body	Murda
Maric (+M) marchi	Pepper	Maric
Marimos (R)	Brawl; fight; fist fighting	Mara mari
Marji; murji (+M)	Will; assent; taking favorably	Marzi
Marot	To finish; to complete	Marot
Marpit	Assault and battery	Marpit
Marsa	Monthly	Mawar
Marsal; maskal (M)	Light; to light; to emit light; to shine	Macal; machel
Martya (R)	Angle of death	Martya; jam; maran har
Maruk	To eat	Murkna
Marur	To decay; to shew signs of decay	Marur (Pb. marur is used for dysentery)
Mas (R)	Meat; flesh	Mas

Mas	A month	Mah; mahina
Masalo (R)	Meat-eating	Masalo
Masari (R)	Butcher	Kasai
Mashe (R)	Fish	Machi
Mashuna (R)	Match	Mcna
Masi (K)	A cow	Masi (mother's sister)
Masi	Christ	Masi
Maski	Cult	Maslik
Maskura	The gums	Masura
Masri (+M)	A cultivated pulse	Mari; masar
Mat (M)	Opinion; wisdom	Mat
Mat	A temple; a monastery	Mat (mostly associated with Buddhist)
Mata (M)	Mature as in fruit	Mata (Pb. commonly agreed agenda)
Matar (M)	A kind of pulse	Matar
Matbor (+M)	Well-to-do; honorable;	Mutabir
Matha	Perverse; lazy; indolent	Matha
Matku; mutkor	Fat and short	Matku
Matlab (M)	Wish; intention; purpose	Matlab
Mato (R)	Drunk; intoxicated	Mad-hoch
Matri	A charm doctor; a master of incantation	Mandri

Maursi (+M) maurasi	Hereditary	Maurosi
Maya	sympathy	maya (it is not maya but myea; sab teri maya)
Mech (M)	Chair	
Mechkok marte; mechkok mante	With a smile	Muskandian
Megra; mogra	A drain pipe; the ridge tiles of a roof	Maghora
Meh danra	The bullock on the left side of a row of bullock treading out grain	Hethla dand (dhga)
Mehnot (M)	Labor	Mihnat
Mehnotia (+M)	Industrious; hard working	Mehnati
Mehran	To demure; to refuse; to decline	Moran
Mei (K)	Mother	Mai
Mej	A table	Mez
Mej	Table	Mej
Mejaj	Temper	Majaj
Mejas	To consult together	Melas
Mejaz (+M)	Temperament; disposition	Mezaj
Mel (+M)	Concord; affection; fondness; harmony; agreement	Mel
Mel (R)	Dirt; earth;	Mel

	soil; filth	
Mela	Fair	Mela
Melcho (R)	Snail	Malap
Mele mele	Numerous; in crowds	Mel; meljor
Mena; manna (R)	No; not	Manna
Meramot	To mend; to repair	Maramat
Merel; meraltar (R)	Die; cease to exist; expire	Marna; maut
Merhao (M)	To twist; to wind	Morao; marorna; marora dena
Merza (R)	Envy; jealousy	Marz
Mesa	Of solitary habits; unsociable	Mesna
Met mat (M)	To settle; to hush up	Muk-muka
Metao (M)	To wipe out	Metao
Meyadi	Terminable period	Meyadi
Miad	Term	Miad
Miad; mead (M) meyad	Term; period	Mead
Miad; mod; mid; moiad (M)	One; single;	Mid; miad
Micha michi	In vain; trifling; without sufficient cause	Masan msan
Mid-ghari (M)	A short while; a moment	Mid-ghari
Mid-mon-te (M)	With one mind	Midmonte
Mihin (M)	Fine	Mihin (delicate)

Mil	Cor. English; a mile	Mil
Milan; milon; milap (+M)	To unite; to join; concord	Milan; milap
Milap	Harmony	Milap
Milau	To mix; to unite; to reconcile	Milau
Mili guti	To arrange; to consult; to scheme	Mili bhagat
Milijili	Union	Miljul
Milijili; miljul; miljol (+M)	Concord; union	Miljul
Miluwil (R)	Extend mercy; feel compassion/ pity	Milul
Milwa milwi	To form an illicit union	Milwa milwi
Mindi (M)	Sheep; one having shaggy hair	Mindi (male minda; or bhidu)
Minha; mina (+M)	To subtract; to deduct	Minha
Mirgi (+M)	Epilepsy	Mirgi
Mirgi jel	A species of deer	Mirg
Mis	To consult together; to plot; to scheme; to conspire	Mith; mithia
Misi (+M)	Hair on the upper lip	Misi; masan
Misi (M)	Black tooth-	Misi

	powder or paste	
Misi juan	A youth or maiden	Misi juan (youth whose masan have started appearing)
Misi	A powder with which the teeth are tinged a black color	Misi
Misil (+M)	The paper or record of a case to act as a magistrate or judge	Misil
Misri (+M)	Sugar candy	Misri
Misri bata	A method of dividing village land so that no person gets two contiguous fields or too much of one quality of land	
Mistri (+M)	A mechanic; a tradesman	Mistri
Mit sae	One hundred	Ik soo
Mit	One; single; to unite; to mix	Mit (Pb. It also means one's turn in playing games)
Mitar	Friend	Mitar
Mitar; mitor	Friend	Mitar
Mitha	sweet	mitha

Mitha; mitho (+M)	Sweet	Mitha
Mithai (+M)	Sweetmeat	Mithai
Mithi	Kind of spice	Methi
Moca	The mouth	Moca
Mocelka (+M) muchilka	Personal recognizance	Mocelka
Mocrao	To eat	Mochna (specifically; as of animals)
Mod; modre	Amidst; from amongst	Mad
Modam	Continuity; always	Madam
Modet; modod (M)	To assist; assistance; help	Madad
Modhobon	A honey forest; a desirable place	Madhoban
Modhom	Middle; intermediate	Madham
Modod	To help; to assist; help	Madad
Modod;Sahaita	Assistance	Madad;Sahaita
Mogoj	Brain	Magaj
Mogol (M)	A Kabuli	Mughal
Mogon	To be astonished. To be amazed; to be merry or careless; as one intoxicated	Magan (absorbed)
Moh (+M)	Pity;	Moh (love)

	compassion	
Moh-jud (M)	To collect; ready	Maujud
Mohlon; mahlon	Medicine for external application	Malam
Mohni (M)	To charm; charming	Mohni
Mohor (+K)	A seal	Mohar
Mohor (+M)	A gold coin	Mohor
Mohor	seal	mohar
Mojlis	Conference	Majlis
Mokabila (M)	To confront	Mukabla
Mokam	Residence	Mokam (stay)
Mokkao	To be speechless	Makko thap
Mokodoma (+M)	A law suit	Mukadma
Mokon	To tire; to finish; to be done	Mukan
Mokoror; mokorora (+M)	Perpetual	Mokarar; mokarara
Mol (+M) (+R)	Price; have value	Mul; mol
Mol (R)	Vine; alcohol	Sharab (Wais Shah uses mol with this meaning in stanza 264)
Molam (+M) molaim	Soft; yielding	Molaim
Molao (M)	To polish; to cleanse by rubbing	Malna
Molari (R)	Vinter	Kalal
Mom (K)	A mixture of fat	Mom

Mom (R)	Wax	Mom
Momeli (R)	A candle	Mom bati
Momjama (K)	A wax cloth	Momjama
Mon (+M)	Mind; spirit	Man
Mon	Mind	Mun
Monadi	To proclaim; to preach	Monadi
Monda	Fall in price; to deteriorate; to go bad	Manda
Mondon	Having no hair on the upper lip	Modon; much monda
Mone (M)	To wish; to think; to consider	Mone
Mophot; muphut (+M)	Free; without payment	Mophat
Mora (M)	Bundle of grain	Bora
Moraba (M)	Aloe	Moraba
Moramet (K)	Repair	Moramat
Morao	Die	Marna
Morca murci	To writhe; to contort; twisting from side to side	Mocora
Morjad (M)	Respect; honor; to respect	Morchad
Morji (M)	Wish; pleasure	Marzi
Morna; moron	Death	Marna
Moron soman	Like death	Maran wanhg
Morot bhui	The dying	Mardi bhoin

	world	(bhomi)
Morsha (k)	A ditch	Morca
Morubi; murubi	An elder; head of the family	Morabi (life sustainer)
Mosa (R)	Orally; verbally	Monh-zabani
Mosa mosa	Sometimes; now and then	Masan masan
Mosal	Torch	Masal
Moskot	Difficulty	Mochakat (very hard work)
Mosmoso	Silent; dejected	Guhmsum
Mosodi	The person through whom the raja or Zamindar communicate with his amla (staff)	Mosodi
Mosokusi	To compel; to force against one's will	Mochakti
Mosola	spice	masala
Mostoram	Careless of what may happen	Mastoram
Mot	Purpose; wish; intent; opinion; method; way; mode	Mat
Mota (+M)	Fat	Mota
Mota	Coarse	Mota

Motaen; motean	To be appointed	Motaen
Moti; muti	Pearl	Moti
Motiao	To appropriate; to take possession of	Mothna
Motlob; matlab	Purpose	Matlab
Mowasi	Cattle	Mowaichi
Mu (+M)	The nose	Pb. nak
Muci (+M)	Shoemaker	Muci
Mudali	Defendant; accused	Mudaaleh
Mudki (K)	A big earthen jar	Matki
Mudoe (+M) mudai	Plaintiff; suitor;	Mudae
Mugi dal	A pulse	Dal mung
Muha muhi (+M)	In front of; face to face	Muha muhi; amne samne
Muhar	To head; direction	Muhar
Muhim; muhin	Danger; difficulty; affliction	Muhim (an adventure; a very difficult goal to set forth)
Muhri	A clerk; a vernacular clerk	Muharar
Mui (R)	Face; mouth	Monh
Muid (K)	A buffalo	Majh
Muja (K)	Stockings; socks	
Mujra (M)	To set off; to deduct	Mujra (Pb. tamasha; gathering around

		dancing girls)
Muk mak (K)	Quickly and roughly	Muk mak; mukmaka
Mukharat; mukharot	By word of mouth	
Mukhia	Leader	Mukhi
Mukhia; mul (M)	Principal; chief	Mukhia
Mukhia;Pordhan	Chief	Mukhia;Pardhan
Mukhia;Purkha	Elder	Mukhi;Purkha
Muklo (R)	Abandoned; deserted	Muka
Mukuph; mukup	To be deferred; postponed; delayed	Maukuph
Mul	Fundamental; real principal	Mul
Mula	A low stool made of plaited canes	Mura
Mula arak	Redish	Muli
Mulaiya	To fix the price of a thing without weighing	
Mulo (R)	Dead; deceased	Muia; murda
Munapha (M)	Profit	Munapha; napha
Munda (+M) mund	Head; end	Munda (Pb. a boy)
Munda mundi	In equal proportions; head for head	Munda mundi
Munda	A tribe	Munda

	inhabiting the Chota Nagpur plateau	
Munda; mundan	To close an opening; hole &c.	Buca
Mundha; mundhat	Stump of a tree	Mudh
Mundla (M)	To crop the hair closely	Mundan; tind
Mundla; mundli	Shaven head (male and female)	Munia; munni (Pb. taindo; taindi)
Mundra (M)	A kind of ear ornament	Mundra
Munga (+M) murai	The horse redish	Muli
Munga suti	The fruit of the Horse redish	Mungra
Munga	Coral	Munga
Munib	Employer; master	Munib
Munjil	A day's journey	Manzil (the destination)
Mur (M)	Principal	Mul
Murad; murat	Respect; honor; wish; intention	Murad
Muragan	Drugs or medicines in general	Pb. Oily; greasy
Murdar (+M)	A corpse	Murdar
Murga	A cock	Murga
Murhut	An image; an idol	Murat

Muri (K)	A drain; a culvert	Muri (a secrete door)
Murkh (M)	Ignorant; obstinate	Murakh
Murli (+M)	A whistle with six or seven finger holes	Murli
Murro (R)	Mine	Mera
Mururi	A veiled name for cholera	Muror
Murut (M)	Image	Murut
Murut	Idol	Murat
Musaphir	A traveller	Musaphir
Mushlia (K)	To meddle with	Maslia; madholia
Musili; musil	A mode of extorting payment of a debt by making the person sit by until he agrees to the terms offered to him	Musuli (Pb. not common practice in Punjab)
Muskil (+M)	Difficult	Muchkil
Musla (K)	Species	Masala
Musla	A Musalman	Musla
Mut (K)	Thinking; to design	Mat
Muta (K)	Rough; coarse	Muta (like muta cawal)
Mutar mutar	Steadfastly; having the	Mutar mutar

	eyes fixed; staring	
Muter (R)	Pee; urine	Muter
Muterdo (R)	Bed-wetter	
Muterdyol (R)	Be urinated on	
Muth (+M)	The measure of the distance from the elbow-joint to the closed fist	Muth
Muth	Fist	Muth
Muthi (+M)	A handle	Muthi
Muthiao (M)	To grasp tightly	Muthiao
Mutka (M)	To strike with clenched fist	Mukka
Mutrel (R)	Urinate	Mutarna
Mutrimos (R)	Piss; urination	Mut
Mutya (R)	Butt (of a rifle)	Muthia; muth
Myntor	A mantra or magic	Mantar
	N	
NA	A popular Punjabi game probably played at Ada by herders. It is played by 4; each with 4 pieces called	Ada khada

	tahniian. In Khasi khada means 12 and a similar game baran tahni is played between two with 12 pieces each	
Na but (R)	Few; not many	Na-buhat
Na (R)	No	Na
Na; nam; nutum	Name	Nan
Nabab (M)	Rich and haughty	Nawab
Nabalok (+M)	Young; under age; immature	Nabalag
Nabalok	Minor	Nabalig
Nabar (K)	From outside; externally	Nabri (as revolt seems a derivation)
Nacao (+M)	The cause to dance	Nacao
Nacao	Dance	Nach
Nacaria; lacar (+M)	Helpless; without resources	Nacar; lacar
Nacnia; naconi (+M)	A dancer	Naci
Nadan; nandhan; nindhan (+M)	Meek; poor; destitute; humble; to despise; to slight	Nadan (With less or no knowledge)
Nadi nala din	The rainy	

	season when the rivers are full	
Naera	A cultivated fiber yielding plant	Narma
Nag (M)	A specie of snake	Nag
Nagad; nogod (+M)	Cash	Nakad
Nagar caker (+M)	Area of village	Nagar caker
Nagar	City	Nagar
Nagar; nangar	A city; large town	Nagar
Nagera (M)	A large drum; to announce by beat of drum	Nagara; nakara
Nagnagin	A species of snake	Pb. Nag; nagan
Nagraha (M)	One who lives in town or city	Nagaria; shehri
Nahak (M)	Fruitless; useless	Nahak (unjust)
Nahan (M)	Bathing ceremony connected with birth; marriage and death	Nahan; nahawan (taking a bath)
Nahar	Canal	Nahar
Naharni	A small instrument containing tweesers ;	Naharni; nehrna

	needle for extracting thorns and knife for cutting nails	
Nahas; tahas nahas	To waste; to squander	Tahas nahas
Nahel	A plough	Hal
Nai (M)	A big river	Nadi
Nai (R)	Finger	Nohn (finger nail; nai must be for finger at sometime)
Naib	A deputy	Naib
Naihar (+M)	Applied to parents house after marriage	Naihar; mape
Naiyarel (R)	Bath	Nahawan; naona
Najar	Look	Najar
Najar; najer (+M)	To see; to look; sight; vision	Nazar
Najarband (M)	To confine	Nazarband
Najom (M)	Witch	Najom (forecasting)
Nak dandi	Bridge of nose	Naka dandi
Nak risa	Nasal polypus	Sind; seend
Nak	A naik; corporal	Naik
Naka	To hang something	Pb. A cut as of in watercourse
Nakabul (+M)	To deny; to refuse assent	Nakabul
Nakal (M)	Copy	Nakal

Nakara	Offensive; polluted; defiled; dirty	Nakara (useless)
Nakarar	To deny	Ankar
Nakatia (M)	One; whose nose has been chopped off	Nakatia
Nakh (R)	Nose	Nak
Nakh-tele (R)	Ashamed; embarrassed	Nak-thele
Nakhali (R)	Nosy	
Nakhe mukhe	Of a good countenance; good looking	Nak nakcha
Nakic	A comb	Kangi
Nakkata	To cut off the nose; to disgrace; to dishonor	Nakkata
Naklaha; naklahi	A pretender	Naklia (Pb. person or group preforming play)
Naksa (+M)	A picture; a representation; a map	Nakcha
Nal (+M)	A horse or bullock shoe	Nal; khurian
Nal	A tube; a pipe	Nal
Nala; nali (+M)	A stream; a ravine; a ditch	Nala; nali; khala
Nala;nali	stream	nala;nali
Nali	Barrel	Nuli
Nalis; lalis (+M)	To complain; to bring an	Nalich

	accusation	
Nam (K) (+M)	Fame; reputation; name	Nan
Nam; na	To seek; to find; to obtain; to get; to wish for	Nam; na
Namn nam; nam namte	All; all without exception	Nam nam
Namuna	Example	Namuna
Namuna; nomona (+M)	Example; pattern	Namuna
Nan (M)	Thin; fine	Nan
Nan bir (M)	A thin jungle	
Nana (+M)	Father's elder sister; aunt	Pb. maternal grandfather
Nande (M)	Close by; near	Lage
Nanga	Naked	Nanga
Nangal	The thong which binds the yoke to the plough beam	
Nangar Jugi	A wandering ascetic	Bhundo jugi
Nangar bhula; nangar bhuli	Wandering (male and female)	Nagar phirtu
Nange (R)	Bare	Nanga
Nange-chuchyango (R)	Bare-breasted; topless	Nangi-chati (cuci is mamma)

Nange-purengo	Bare-footed	Nange-pair
Nangimos (R)	Nudity; nakedness	Nang-dharang
Nango-bulako (R)	Wretchedly poor	Nanga-bhukha
Nani (M)	Grand mother	Nani
Nanjom	A witch	Najom (future forecasting; for witch Pb. dain; curel)
Nano (R)	Father's brother; uncle	Nano (mother's father)
Nanula (R)	Boot	Nal (horse's nal)
Nao (M)	A boat	Nao
Nao Thikan	Residence address	Nan thikana
Naogao	Residence address	Pb. Sarnawan
Naokar	A servant	Naokar
Naokri	Service	Naokri
Nap; napti (+M)	To measure	Nap
Napac	Absence of blemish; disfiguremen t; deformity;	Napak
Naparh (M)	Illiterate	Anparh
Napha; lapha (+M)	Profit	Napha
Napit	Barbar	Nai
Nar khunti	Part of the weaver's loom; the posts which support the roller on	

	which the cloth is wound as woven	
Nara	A kind of ear ornament	Kanta
Naraj (+M)	Displeased; to become poor	Naraz
Narak; narok (+P)	Excrement; filth	Narak
Narandja (R)	Orange	Naranji
Narangi (+M)	An orange	Narangi
Narangi	orange	narangi;sangtra
Nari thuri	Only; entirely	Niri
Nari	The pulse at the wrist	Nar; nabaz
Narjor (+M)	Relationship by marriage	Narjor (Naris woman and jor is relationship; Pb. wiah)
Narom; naram; narna; narmi; normanorum (+P) narma	Soft	Naram; narma(a specie of cotton)
Nas (+M) nast	To destroy; to ruin; to annihilate	Nas
Nas (R)	Was not	Nahin
Nase	Untrue; false	Nase
Nashlo (R)	Eloped; deserted	Nasna (nas jana)
Nashr (M)	Water channel	Pb. to publicize
Nashti (R)	Cannot; could not	Nahin
Nasib; naseb (+M)	Fate	Naseb

Nasib;Mahabhag	Luck	Nasib;Bhag
Nasor	Deep wound	Nasor (deep wound)
Nasti	To render nul and void; to deny; to annihilate	Nasti (Pb. it is also used for laziness)
Nasul (R)	Bad; dangerous; harmful	Nas (like nas huna)
Nasulimos (R)	Tribulation; trouble; woe	Satianas
Nat khatia (M)	Naughty; rouge	Natkhat
Nata; nata suta (+M)	Temporary relationship; to contact	Nata
Nath; nat; nathni	To bore a bullock nose and put in a string with which to guide him; a nose ring	Nath (Pb. it is also used by nose ornament of women and for controlling)
Nathi	A bundle of papers [attached with eachother)	Nathi
Nathni; nath (M)	Nose ring	Nath
Nati (+M)	A grnadchild	Nati (used in Hindi)
Natua	Dom dancer	Natua; naca
Naturanalo (R)	As usual	Nit
Natwa	A winder on which the	

	thread on the spindle of the spinning wheel is wound; to wind thread off the spindle on to a (natwa)winder	
Nau (+M) Naua	Barber	Nai
Naukar;dasi	servant	naukar;dasi
Nav (R)	Name; identity	Nan; nawan
Nawa (+M)	New; fresh	Nawan
Nawa	New	Nanwan
Ne	Presently; in no long time; very recently	Hune
Ne-re; nende; netare (M)	Here; in this; in this place	Nere
Neae; neao	To judge; to settle a dispute	Nean (justice)
Neec (M)	Low; mean	Neec
Neg; nego (R)	Instead of; rather than	Sagon
Neh (K)	To remain; to stick to	Neh (love; the base on which a structure is built)
Nehal	To do; to accomplish	Nehal (to be refreshed)
Nehali	Of no use; unable to work; not	Badhali (Pb. nihali is comforter as

	able to earn anything.	well)
Nehor (+M)	To beseech; to plead; to implore	Nehora; henora
Nel; (+M) lel	To see; to look; to consider; to appear; to seem	Nel (Pb. original meaning lost and now simply means blue color or tree. However; in verses like â€œnil kraian nelkanâ€ it may mean to see)
Nemar (M)	Meek; gentle; good-natured	Nemana
Nemos	To become assuaged as anger; to be appeased; to be allayed	Namos (honor; but it may be a different word)
Neo (M)	Foundation	Neo; nenh
Neota (+M)	To invite	Neota; roti warjna
Nepata (R)	Niece ; granddaught er	
Nepoto; nipoto (R)	Nephew	
Nevo-avilo (R)	Newly arrived	Nawan Aiya
Nevo; nevi (R)	New; newcomer	Nawan
Nevorro (R)	Brand new	Nawan nakor
Newan	Bent; curved; to bend; to curve	Newan (Pb. lower surfaced cultivation field)
Ngun (K)	With the	Ngun (like in

	head bent down	sarngun)
Nia (K)	Reason; argument	Nia (Nian as justice)
Niam	Covenant	Nem
Nibar (M)	Weak	Lacar
Nibasi	Inhabitant	Basi
Nibhao (M)	To spend time	Nibhao (tolerating to spend time)
Nichanaha; nichanahi	Bothersome; annoying (male and female)	Candra
Nichora; nichura	Unalloyed; faultless; unmixed; entirely; without admixture; pure	Narol
Nichura	To squeeze	Nicura
Nicind; nicit (+M)	Without care or anxiety	Nicind; nicit
Nico	Low; scandalous; unbecoming	Nic (nican; plural)
Nidaria (M)	Fearless	Nadar
Nidhan; nindhan; nindau	To despise; to slight; to revile	Nindhan
Nihai	An anvil	Aeran
Nihait (M)	Absolutely mean; low; to hate; to despise	Nikhid

Nij (M)	To open	Nij
Nij; nije; niji (+M)	Private; one's own; original	Niji
Nijat	Without any recognized caste; having been out-casted	Nijat (nejat also means freedom)
Nijgut	For certain; by oneself; at first hand	Naji
Nijojor; nijor	Weak; feeble; poor	Kamzor
Nikas (+M)	Outlet opening; to make up an account	Nikas
Nikas	outlet	nikas
Nikhar	Entirely; altogether; in full recovered from illness; refreshed	Nikhar
Nikhora	Pure	Nikhora
Niki badi (+M)	Good and evil	Naki badi
Nikol	A copy	Nakal
Nikti tula	Small scales used to weigh precious metals like gold and silver	Nikti tula; niki tula
Nilaj; nilajia (+M)	Shamelessness	Nilaj
Nilam (M)	To sell by	Nilam

	auction	
Nim (+M)	A common small tree whose leaves and figs are used as medicine and as a tooth brush	Nim
Nimak Haram; nimok haram	Disloyal; wicked; ungrateful	Namak haram
Nimbha; nibha; nirbha	To bring through ; to stand by in worst circumstances	Nibah
Ninda (M)	To blame	Nindan
Ninda cando	The moon	Can; canda
Ninda	Night; to become night	Ninda (Pb. nind; sleep)
Nindan	Estimating roughly	Nindan
Nindra; nidra	Drowsiness	Nindra
Nindri; nari	The windpipe	Nari
Nir	To disappear as the moon; to flee; to run	Nir (without)
Nira; nirala; nirola	Pure; unadulterated; unalloy	Nira; nirala
Nirai	Peace; without care or anxiety	Nirai
Niral (M)	Beautiful	Narol (pure)

Niras	To be disappointed; to be without hope	Niras
Nirbhoe	Fearless	Nirbhai
Nirbis	Poisonous	Nirbis
Nirbodh (M)	Foolish	Nirbodh
Nirbuj (M)	Slow to understand	Nirbuj (nir-bujh)
Nirdae (M)	Pitiless	Nirdae
Nirdae; nirdae	Absolutely; altogether; totally; completely	Nirdai
Nirdhand; nirdhandi; nirdhok	Without care or anxiety	Nirdhand
Nirdos	Faultless	Nidos
Nirdos; nirdosi; nirdus (+M)	Faultless; blameless; innocent; not guilty	Nirdus
Nirghim	Depressed; dispirited; disfigured by grief &c.	
Nirik; nirikh; niruk; nirukh	Rate; price	Nirikh
Nirmoli	A kind of fruit employed to clear water	Nirmoli (Nim leaves boiled)
Nisa (+M)	An intoxicant; or narcotic; such as opium; ganja; alcohol &c.	Nisha (complete satisfaction; intoxicating)
Nisa	Intoxicants	Nasha

Nisan (+M)	A mark; as on a target; to make a mark	Nishan
Nisan	Mark	Nisan
Nisana	Token	Nisan
Niscae	Certainly; truly; without doubt	Niscae
Niskapat; niskapot	Without deceit; sincere	
Nisun (M)	Void; soundless	Nisun
Nit; nitok (+M) nit	Now; at the moment; to fix; to decide; to settle; to determine	Nit (Pb. forever; over and over; repeatedly)
Niti; net (M)	Conduct; dealing	Niti; net
Nojor	Gaze	Najar
Nokoe	This; this particular one	Nokoe
Nokol;Utrau	Copy	Nakal
Nokor (+M) chakar	Servant	Nokor
Noksan (M)	Damage; loss	Noksan
Nol	A pipe	Nol
Nosto	To destroy; to ruin; to waste	Nosto
Num	Name	Nam
	O	
Oaris	Helper; owner; heir;	Waris

	claimant	
Od	To shelter; to protect; to hide	Od; orh
Odasi (M)	Churned curd	Lassi
Odo; Hado (M)	And; more; moreover	Hoor; aur
Odra udri	Chipped here and there	Odra (From Odherna)
Ojra	Carelessly dressed; cloth or string around the waist	Ojra
Okaj; okajua	Useless; worthless; unserviceable	Okaj
Olo; ondo	Ignorant; foolish	Ulo
Omor	Immortal	Amar
On; an	Grain	An
Ona	That	Ohnan
One	That; which; that	One
Oneao	Unjust	Aneao
Onge (M)	To blow with mouth	Onge
Onka; onkan	Like that	Onkan
Onman	To consider; to deliberate; to estimate; to think	Onman
Onpani	Food and drink	Onpani
Onte	Over there	Othe
Ontor	Mind; heart	Antar; andar

Oprad; opradi	A fault; a crime; guilty; criminal	Oprad; opradi
Opral (R)	Above; on top of; up there	Upar
Opre (R)	Upwards; upstairs	Uprala
Orak	A house; a dwelling place; home	Orak (Pb. towards the end)
Orec	To tear; to rend; to cut	Orec
Oroj	A petition; a representation	Arzi
Ortho	Meaning	Arth
Osot	Untrue; false	Osot
Oste	Slowly; carefully	Ahista
Othar (R)	From there	Odron
	P	
Pac	To make an incision; in surgery	Pach
Pacak	Digestive	Pacna
Pacao (+M)	To digest	Pacao
Pacar (+M)	A wedge driven into a wooden pin	Pacar
Pace; pase	Perhaps	Bhawin, pahwin
Pach pache; pachor	One after the other	Picha piche
Pacha (R)	Peace; safety	Baca
Pacha	To follow up;	Picha (karna)

	to trace; to track	
Pachil	The back part	Pichal (Pochil; as tail).
Pachim (+M)	The west	Pachim
Pachim	West	Pacchim
Pachla (M)	Hinder part	Pichla
Pachla	Backwards	Picche
Pachla; pacla; pachuau; pacuau	To recede; to draw back; to give way; to shrink; to abandon; to withdraw	Piche; pichla
Pachmahi	Belonging to the west	Pachmi
Pachtao; (+M) paschanttap	To be sorry; to grieve; to repent	Pachtao
Padhua; parhua	Educated; lazy	Padhia
Padna; padni (+M)	Given to passing wind; suffering from flatulence	Padna; padni (pad marna)
Paeda (+M)	To give birth to; to produce	Paida
Paemana	A measure	Paimana
Paera; paeraha; paerahi	To swim; swimmer (male and female)	Terna; terak; terakan
Paere	An overflow channel of	Parhi; bhari

	tank &c.	
Paesa; poesa (+M)	A pice; one fourth of an anna	Pesa
Paethan; paethani	A pathan (male and female)	Pathan; pathani
Pagal	Demented	Pagal
Pagal; pagol; pagla	Mad; demented; crazy	Pagal
Pagil	Mad	Pagal
Pahakat	Only	Phakat
Pahal (M)	Iron ploughshare	Phala
Pahalwan	A wrestler	Pahalwan
Pahara; pahra	A guard; a watchman;	Pahro
Pahat	Side; strip; piece; direction	Pasa
Pahi; pera; kupul (M)	A guest	Pahi (Pb. a traveler)
Pahichan (M)	To recognize	Pachan; pehchan
Pahil	First; foremost; before; in time or place	Pahil
Pahil;Pardhan	First	Pahla
Pahilutha	First born	Pahlutha
Pahla pahli	For the first time	Pahla; pahli
Pahna	To make the first sale of the day for cash	

Pahpaha	First sign of the dawn approachin	Poh phutna
Pahra (M)	To guard; to watch	Pahra
Pahrau	To put on the person as a garment; ring; ornament &c.	Pahnau; pahrau
Pahraua	That which has been put on the person; as a garment; ring &c.	
Pahta	Side; strip; piece; direction	Pasa
Pai (K)	A number; small measure of money	Pai
Pai (R)	Water	Pani
Paikar	A trader; one who sells and buy things	Beopar
Paila	A measure; 2 pesa	Dhela
Paji (+M)	A scoundrel	Paji
Paka paki (+M)	To establish an agreement or proposition so that no doubtor subject of	Paka paki

	dispute can remain	
Paka	ripe	paka
Paka; paki	Ripe; efficient; thorough; full; complete; sure; certain	Paka; paki
Pakar	To seize; to take; to catch	Pakar
Pakh (R)	Wing; fin	Pakh; par
Pakha (K)	Fan	Pakha
Pakha (M)	A niche used in a wall as shelf	Ala
Pakka	Incontrovertible	Pakka
Pako (R)	Ripe	Paka
Pakre	To hunt up; to search for	Pakre
Pakro; paktu; pokra; Pukto	Mature; full grown; ripe; strong; able bodied; skilled; efficient	Pak pug
Pal (+M)	A ploughshare	Phala
Pal	A herd; a flock	Pal (Pb. a line; a row)
Pal; palak (M)	In twinkling of an eye; a moment	
Pala (R)	After; behind	Picha (seems from pal as a

		que)
Pala	Frost	Pala
Palak (+M)	Spinach	Palak
Palak	spinach	palak
Palan	A saddle of the native variety for a horse or a pack bullock	Palan
Palao	To nourish; to bring up; as a child	Palna
Palao;Posao	Nourish	Pal Pos
Pale (R)	Afresh; again	Val; phair; bhale
Pale	If; if ever; perhaps	Pale; bhale
Palek	Almost; peradventure	Palek
Pali (+K)	Turn; shift	Pali; wari
Pali pasari; pali pasarite	By turns; in rotation	
Palki (M)	A palanquin	Palki; doli
Palki	palankin	paki
Palpal	Numerous	Palpal (every moment)
Pan (+M)	A leaf chewed by some; betel leaves	Pan
Pana (+M)	Water having raw sugar dissolved in it	Pana (Pb. an instrument used by ironsmiths)
Panc	Five	Panj
Panc; panchahit; pocahit (+M)	An assembly; a council; generally	Pancait

	applied to collective arbitration	
Panda (+M) pandit	A Brahman resident in a temple	Panda; pandit
Pande (M)	A writer; an advisor; a learned person	Pande
Pande	Body region over the symphysis pubes	Paido
Pandrahi; Pandra; Pandri	Greyish colored; applied to buffalos	Peli
Pandu	To become yellow as leaves; to become greyish	Pandu (Mahabharata character)
Pangah (K)	To jolt; to dissent; to move the head from side to side	Pangah
Pani (R)	Water	Pani
Pani	Water	Panni
Panja	Foot mark; foot print	Panja
Panjar	A part of the body in which ribs are	Pinjar
Pao	Feet	Pair
Pap (+K) (+M)	Sin	Pap

Pap; papa; papo (R)	Grandfather	Dada
Papi	sinful	papi
Papi; papin; papia; papiahi (+M)	Sinful; miserly; stingy	Papi; papan
Papor	Cor. English pauper	Papar
Papuchyari (R)	Shoemaker	Mochi (Papuch is a Persian word)
Papusha (R)	Doll; puppet; child's toy	Patola
Par	Relief; escape; refuge; across	Par (usually used for going across but seems it meant going beyond danger)
Para (K)	Younger brother or sister	Para (brother; a Punjabi pronunciation of bhra)
Para	Mercury	Para
Parab	Anniversary	Parb
Paraho; parahua; padhua (+M)	To study; educated	Parhna
Paramesor (M)	God	Parmechwar
Parao	To be; to befall; to fall into or on	Parao; Parne (Pb. used like â€˜sir parne digia)
Parapat	Advantage; benefit	Parapat (to gain)
Parca	Acquaintance; to be known to each other	Pareca; jan pichan; tuaraf
Parcao	To increase; to spread	Parcao (parcar is derived from this; Pb. to coax;

		to appease as a child)
Parcha (M)	A preliminary record of rights	Parca
Parchar (M)	To preach	Parcar
Parda	Curtain	Parda
Pardesi (M)	A foreigner	Pardesi
Pardhan (M)	A chief	Pardhan
Pardnoi (R)	Tailor	Darzi (Pardnoi from parda)
Pargana (+M)	A division of a country; or an estate; generally for fiscal purposes	Pargana
Parha panch	A body of arbitrators; a jury	Parha panc
Parhao	Teach	Parhona
Pari	Turn	Bari
Pari; pari pari (+M)	Turn; by turns	Wari; wari wari
Paria (M)	Time; period	Pb. parar; year before last
Pariare	The four pieces of wood forming the framework of a bed; chair &c.	Pawe
Parikha; porikha	To test; to examine; to prove	Parkhna

Parja (M)	A raiyat; a tenant; masses	Parja
Parkom	A bed	Palang
Parno (R)	Pale; pallid	Pandu (as in Mahabharat)
Parom (M)	Across; beyond; on the other side	Par
Parosi; arose parosi; ar parsoi (+M)	Neighbors	Parosi; arose parosi
Parpao	To burn clearly and brightly	Barkao
Parsao	To distribute cooked food	Parosna
Partap (M)	Power; courage; influence	Partap
Parwana	A written letter	Parwana
Pas	Cor. English pass	Pas
Pas; apas (+M)	Side	Side; neighborhood
Pasa (K)	Luck	Pasa (luck in gambling)
Pasar (M)	To graze cattle in the morning	Pasar (the root word)
Pasar pasat	To be in disorder; to be disarranged; to be topsy	Pasara

	turvy	
Pasar pusur	To whisper	Pasar pusur
Pasar	Expand	Pasar
Pasari (R)	Market place	Pasari (Shop selling herbs &c.)
Pasari; paseri (+M)	Five seers in weight	Paseri (panj seri)
Pase (M)	To entrap; to catch in the net	Phaia
Pash (R)	Half	Pash (do-pash)
Pasi	Noose	Phansi
Pasi; phasi	A running knot; a nose; to snare by a nose; to hang by a nose	Pasi; phasi
Pasind (M)	To approve; to prefer	Pasind
Pasir	To break up and spread on a hard surface; to fly off; as sparks; spray; to spatter &c.	Pasir (Pb. pasrna is stubbornly lying around)
Pasna pasni	To spread here and there	
Pasnga (+M)	Anything put in one scale to equalize it with the other	Pasko
Pasrao (M)	To spread; to extend	Pasrao

Pasu (+M) pasur	An animal; cattle	Pasu
Pat	A lesson	Pat; sabak
Pat Jhar	Autumn	Pat jhar
Pat jhara	Autumn when leaves fall	Pat jhara
Pat marte; pat mente; phat marte; phat mente	Suddenly; without warning	Phata phat
Pat son	Fiber of patson	Patson (Pb. called son only)
Pat	A wedge driven into anything	Pat
Pat;Pata	Leaf	Pat;Pata
Pata (+M)	A lease	Pata
Pata	A primitive kind of oil press	
Patal puri	The nether world	
Patal	Deep in the bowls of the earth	Patal
Patao	To exchange flowers in token of friendship	Patao (to allure; to charm; to draw)
Patar	A sheet or piece of iron beaten out till it is thin	Patra
Patas; patas patus	Sounding of a slap; succession of	Patas (leather hand held piece of leather used

	slapping sounds	by Bhands)
Pate (M)	To wrap up anything round the waist	Pata
Pate (R)	Really	Pata (hon)
Patha	A young he-goat	Patha (assistant or pupil of a wrestler or gangster)
Pathaona	To send	Bajhwana
Pathar (K)	The width and stretch of a ford or stream; thoughtless; heedless	Pathar
Pathe	To bind around the loins	Pathe (To make bread by hand or to make dung cakes; called pathian)
Pathe	To one side; along the edge	Pathe
Pathi	She-kid	Pathi (also she-goat)
Pathra	A stone plate	Pathra
Pati Dhiri	A broad flat stone on which spices are ground	Sil
Pati	A line; a row; a strip	Pati
Patia (+M) pati	A mat	Pati

Patka patki (M)	To throw each other on the ground	Patka patki
Patka	A narrow strip of homemade cloth worn on a turban	Patka (Pb. A piece of cloth put on the shoulder)
Patla	Thin	Patla
Patpal	Branches	Pat
Patpatao; patpotuk	Cracking; patterning	Patpatao
Patra panji; patri panji	An almanack by which Brahmans foretell the future	Patri
Patrin (R)	Leaf	Patar
Patsina (R)	Skate	Phislna
Patta	Lease	Patta
Patta; patti	A leaf	Patta; patti
Patwa	Wanton; lecherous	Lucha
Pauchi; paunchi	A ridge of earth; to make a ridge	Pb. paunci (an ankle ornament)
Pawa (M)	Legs of a bedside or chair; a measure of Â¼	Pawa
Paya	A deep and long poll in river	
Pe (R)	On; at; by; for; per	Pe

Peada (+M)	A messenger who goes on a foot; a peon	Peada
Peaj (+M) peaju	Onion	Peaz; gande
Pear (M)	To love	Pear
Pech (M)	Screw; a difficult situation	Pec
Peckas (+M)	A screw driver	Peckas
Peecha; picha	To follow up; to prosecute a search	Peecha
Pehlan	To start; to move suddenly;	Pehal
Pejlec; hejlec	Dirty; untidy	Paleet
Pekel (R)	Bake; broil; cook; fry; roast	Pakana; bhunana
Pekitori (R)	Cook	Bawarci
Peko (R)	Baked; cooked	Pakwan
Pelivoniya (R)	Wrestling; wrestling match	Pehlwan; palwan; balwan
Penc	A screw; narrow; crowded; difficulty	Pec
Pend	A patch	Pewand; taki
Penda (+M)	The bottom; base; underpart	Penda
Pengha	To pretend	Pengha (fissure)

	ignorance	
Penhao (M)	To induce a cow to let down the milk	Pasmao
Peprec	To fill	Peran; bharan
Pera	A kinsman; a relative; to show hospitality; to visit	Prohna
Pere (M)	To fill	Bharna
Perosan; person; phersao	To jump or bound; to fall; to roll; as one in a recumbent position	Prechan
Perta	Perverse; having a twist; unsociable	Perta
Pervimata (R)	Priorities	Pahal
Pes (+M)	To present; as a petitioner complaint	Pech
Pesen pesen (M)	To ooze out in small quantities	Pesen; sen (pesena is derivation)
Peskar (+M)	The official whose duty is to lay petitions before the magistrate	Pechkar
Peski	An advance	Pechgi

	of pay	
Pesrao	To overcome; to conquer	Pesrao
Pet	The belly; the stomach	Pet
Petari; petara	A kind of a round bamboo basket with a lid	Petari; petara
Petdandia; petlaha; petposa	As pet	Pet
Petec	To snip off	Petej
Peti (M)	A bamboo basket with a lid	Pb. Big trunk or iron box
Petposa (M)	Selfish and greedy	Petpalan
Petu (M)	Greedy	Petu (one who easts too much)
Pha (K)	To risk; to jeopardize; to hazard	Pha (hanging; getting trapped)
Phad	A crowd; an army	Phauj
Phada	Open; unfenced; unenclosed	Phada
Phadda	To kick	Thuda
Phaddari; phaudari; phaujdari	Criminal case	Phaujdari
Phaeda (M)	Benefit; profit	Phaeda
Phaeda	Profit; benefit	Phaeda
Phael; phaela; phaelao	Broad; wide;	Phael; phaela;

	ample; extensive; spacious; expansive	phaelao
Phagua	Belonging to moth of Phagan	Phagua
Phagun	February	Phagan
Phajil	Over and above what is necessary; srplus	Phazil
Phak (R)	Wing; fin	Phank; par
Phak	Open and free space	Phank (empty; penniless)
Phaki	To deceive; to trick; to play one false	Phakri
Phakir	Faker; beggar; religious medicant; poor; destitute	Phakir
Phakki; phaki; paki; phakni	A medicine in powder	Phakki
Phakphak	Extremely hungry	Phakphak
Phakua	Deceitful; tricky	Pakhandi; phakar
Phal (R)	Broad; plank	Phalia
Phal	Fruit	Phal
Phal; phol	All kinds of fruits; result; recompense	Phal phol
Phalna; phalni (+M)	A certain or a	Phalana; phalani

	particular person (male and female	
Phalti	Extra	Phaltu
Phalti; phaltu (+M)	Disengaged; extra; superfluous; inrrelevant	Phalti; phaltu
Phand	Wide; broad	Phand
Phand; phanda (+M)	A noose; a net; a trap; to ensnare	Phand; phanda
Phanda	To kick; to kick with the hind feet	Phanda; phandna (to give a severe beating)
Phandao (M)	To bind together; to join together	Phandao
Phandavel; phandado (R)	To be enclosed; arrested	Phadna; pharna
Phandel (R)	Tie; knot	Phand
Phandel	Over and above what is necessary; srplus	Phalto
Phando	Distress; perplexity; difficulty	Phandia
Phandra	Wide apart; as the bars of a cage	
Phank (M)	Open; open space	Phank (Pb. penniless; empty pocket)
Phanrr (R)	Silk	Phar

Phansi (M)	A nose; killing by hanging	Phansi
Phaph	To boast; to blow; an exaggerator	Phapha (as used in phaph e kutna or kutni)
Phara (M)	A piece; to cut up into pieces	Phara
Pharak	Distance; difference; distinction;	Pharak
Pharak;Dur	Distance	Pharak;Dur
Phareb (+M)	To trick; to deceive	Phareb
Pharep (K)	To make a false charge; or complaint against a person	
Phari (R)	Pregnant; heavy	Bhari
Phari	The shoulder; the shoulder meat	Phari
Pharia (K)	To split into small pieces	Pharia
Pharian	To separate the threads; to disentangle	Pharian (segments of as in orange)
Pharkan (M)	At a distance; off; away	Pharkan (Phrak is derivation)
Pharkao (M)	To separate; to take away	Pharkao; pharkna
Pharkao	To fly; to flee	Pharkao (To kill; to beat; to take

		on the target)
Pharla (R)	Brothers	Para; bhara
Pharma	Mould	Pharma
Pharmao; phormao (+M)	To recognize; to order	Pharmao (respectfully asking other to say something)
Pharmas; phormas	To give an order for anything to be made	Pharmaich (To ask or request for a special favor)
Pharo (R)	Heavy; difficult; arborous	Bhara
Pharphar (+M)	To talk glibly; to chatter;	Pharphar
Pharpharao	To tear; to make a long tear; as in cloth	Pharna
Pharpharia (+M)	Glib; Non-cohesive; detached; loose	Phapharia
Pharrado (R)	Broken up; shattered	Phatia; pharia
Pharsi; parsi	Language; Persian	Pharsi
Phasad; phesud (+M)	Violence; crime	Phasad
Phasal; phosol	Crop; harvest	Phasal
Phasao (M)	To entrap; to entangle	Phasao
Phasi	A noose; a loop; to noose; to	Phasi

	strangle; to snare; to kill by hanging	
Phasiara	Deceitful; tricky; hypocritical	Phasiara; phasao
Phasur phasur (M)	To whisper	Phasur phasur
Phatak ; phatok (+M)	A large gate; to shut in; to deprive one of his liberty	Phatak
Phatao	To become sour; to go bad; to curdle; as milk	Phatna
Phataphat	Suddenly; distressing; severe; in close succession	Phataphat
Phati	To clear; to clean	Phati (like in po phati)
Phatkao	To sift; to wnow; to dust; to shake or knocking off anything adhering; as dust &c.	Phatkao; chatkao
Phatkar	To vomit	Phatkar (to curse; appearing of ugliness on face)
Phatoe	A sleeveless waistcoat	Phatoe

Phatok	Gate	Phatak
Phaud (M)	A large assembly; an army	Phauj
Phaudari (M)	Criminal; relating to criminal	Phaujdari
Phauti	Extra; unoccupied; ownerless; unemployed; not in use; surplus; graits	Phoka; phoki
Phaaá[1]-kar	To vomit	phaaá[1]-kar (Pb. To show ugly face; to have been cursed)
Pheca	The hip	Picha
Phecan	To backbite; to slander behind one's back	Phecan; pharphej
Phed	Near; close; low; the bottom of lowest part of anything; base; foot	Painda
Phen phen	To grumble; to complain	Phen phen
Phen; pher	Again; change; turn; circumference	Pher
Phenkao	To be lost; to stray; to	Bhulekha

	conceal	
Pher (K)	To differ	Pher
Pher	Change	Pher
Pherdo (R)	Filled up; full; complete	Bharia; bharpur
Pheroi (M)	To trade by carrying goods	Pheri
Phet (K)	To run	Phut (phutna)
Phet; phetao (+M)	To mix; to beat; as an egg; to shuffle as cards	Phetna (also beating a person)
Phetar	A heifer	Phandar
Phiah (K)	To split	Phiah (to crush)
Phikir (K) (+M)	To take pains to do a thing; to be in earnest; a hermit; a beggar	Phikir (a hermit; a beggar)
Phikir	Thought; reflection; consideration	Phikir
Phira (K)	To guard; to watch	Phira
Phiran	To restore; to give back; to return	Phiran
Phiravdo (R)	Nomadic; traveling	Phirtu
Phiriadi; phuriadi;	An accuser; a complainant; a plaintiff	Phiriadi
Phirka	Stratagem	Phirka (sect)

Phirki	A door; a window opening	Phirki
Phit	To reject; defective; imperfect	Phit
Phita (+K) (+M)	Tape; braid; wick of lamp; a band of plaited hair; used by women to tie up the hair	Phita
Phiti	A skein of thread	Phiti
Phitkari	Alternate	Phitkari
Phitkiri (+M)	Alum	Phatkiri
Phlan (K)	To flatter; to cheat; to pretend	Phalona
Phna (K)	To fasten a door with two cross bolts	Phana
Phogra; Phugri	Having lost the front teeth; toothless (male and female)	Bora; bori
Phohom; pohom (+M)	To recognize; to see distinctly	Phaham
Phoidari (K)	Criminal case	Fojdari
Phoka (+M)	To blister; to rise in a blister	Phora

Phoka	Blister	Phoda
Phoki (M)	Empty	Phoki
Phokti	Humorous; joking	Phabti; jugat
Phoktia; phuktia	A humorist; a comical fellow	Phabtia; jugtia
Phol; pholao	Fruit; to bear fruit	Phal; phalao
Pholok (M)	Soft	Phulka
Pholon	Increase	Phulan
Phond	Malign	Bhand
Phophuda; phuphunda (M)	Rotten; mildew; moldy	Phuphunda
Phosal	Harvest	Phasal
Phot (K)	Cutting sharp	Phat
Phub (R)	Pus; suppuration	Pas; peep (phora is derivation from phub)
Phudna	An ornament of cotton or silk thread	Phundana
Phuhi; puhi	To rain gently; to drizzle	Phuhi; phawar
Phuk	To breath quickly and heavily	Phuk
Phukar (M)	To call; referring especially to the calling up of court cases	Pukar
Phukar	An opening; an aperture;	Phukar; phukni

	a hole through and through as in a wall; a chimney opening	
Phuki	Empty; hollow;	Phuki; phooki
Phukni	Blowpipe	Phukni
Phul	Flower	Phul
Phulbaria	A flower garden	Phulwari
Phunda; phundina (M)	An ornamental cotton band worn around the waist or arm	Phundina
Phupha (M)	Father's sister's husband	Puphar
Phur (+M)	To eject from the mouth as the stone of a fruit; to snort	Phur
Phuran	To fine; to mulet	Phuran (to get success by chance)
Phuranes; Phuranimos (R)	In the old way; antiquity	Purana
Phurdimos (R)	Breath; gasp; puff	
Phuri (R)	Elderly lady	Bhuri
Phursat; phursut (+M)	Leisure; opportunity	Phursat

Phurti (+M)	Quickly; rapidly	Phurti
Phus (R)	Straw; thatched	Phus
Phus	Trivial	Phus (to turn into nothing)
Phuski (M)	To whisper	Phuski
Phuslao (M)	To entice; to flatter; to coax; to lead astray	Phuslao
Phusphas; phasphus	Very slightly; very small in quantity	Phusphas
Phut (K) (+M)	To uproot; to break; to burst	Phut; putna
Phut	A kind of a melon	Phut
Phut;Khergunja	Melon	Phut;Kharbuja
Phuta phuti (+M)	To separate; to disperse; each to go his own way	Phuta phuti
Phutau	To spring; to burst; to make public	Phutao
Phutia (M)	Small coins; copper pieces	Phutia; bhan
Phutoi (K)	Waistcoat	Phatoi
Phuv (R)	Earth; country; ground; land; holding; property	Phavi; bhoin
Pia; piau	Closely fit; to	Pia; piau

	be in close friendship	
Piada (K)	A peon	Piada
Piak; piakar (+M)	Greatly addicted to liquor ; a drunkard	Piak
Picha; piche (+M)	As often as every time	Picha
Pichan; paechano	To perceive; distinguish; to recognize; to identify	Pichan
Pichar	Too far back; as a load on a cart	Pichar
Pichauri	A large cotton shawlplaid; gently made by sewing two or more width of cloth together	
Pichkari; phocor		
Pichlau	To slip; to take a false step	Phislna
Pichol	To slip; to slide; to ignore; to take note of	Phislna
Picir	To spray	Picir marna
Picir; picir picir	To fly off; as small chips of wood from an axe; or	Picir picir

	water falling on a hard surface ; to splash	
Picopocomarte	Weak; inferior; below par	Pichokar
Pilsin; pinsin	Pension; pencil	Pilsin; pinchan
Pind	An altar; a small raised platform for the purpose of the altar	Pind (village)
Pinda	A raised platform round a house occupying the space between the wall and the drip of the caves	Pinda (body)
Pipa (+K) (+M)	A barrel	Pipa
Pipni	The eyelash	Pipni
Piprian	A butterfly	Titli
Piramni (R)	Girlfriend; lover	Premni; premka
Pirhi (+M)	A generation	Pirhi
Pirhi	A cushion of wood on which a beam rests	Pirhi (A small stole to sit on)
Piri	A small round basket for keeping	Pitari

	snakes	
Pirit (+M)	Affectionate; friendly; love	Pirit (love)
Pirthi; pirthimi (+M)	The world	Pirthwi
Pirus	Beestings or first milk given by the cow after calving	Bohli
Pisar pasar	Loose; loosely; non-cohesive; slack	Pisar ; pisria
Pit	The gall; anger; wrath	Pit
Pitari; Tukri	Basket	Pitari; Tokri
Pitau (+M)	To beat with the hand or any implement or hammer	Pitau; pitna
Pitet	To card or tease cotton with a bow	Pitet, jhmbna
Pitol	Brass	Pital
Pituk	A glutton	Pitu; Paitu
Piuri (+M)	To make little hollow rolls of cotton to be spun into thread	Puni
Piyal; pel (R)	Drink	Piyal
Pleit (K)	Plate	Plate
Po (R)	On	Upar
Poa (M)	To break into small pieces	Poa

Pocoe	Liquor made from rice	Pich (thickened water of boiled rice)
Pod	A little	Pod (new generation)
Podina	Mint	Pudina
Podo (R)	Bridge	Pul
Podor	Dry	Dry
Poha	A shoot springing from the ground; seeding of a tree	Poha
Pohom	To recognize; to discern; to see distinctly	Pehcan; mafhom
Pohrao; Pahrau	To put on; as cloths; ornaments; ; rings &c.	Pahrao; pahnao
Pohre pohre	From time to time	Pehar pehar
Pokhao	To rear; to bring up; to nourish	Palo
Pokta; pokto	Strong; hard; substantial; seasoned	Paka
Polok; polokh	An instant	Palak
Pontha	To devise; to arrange; to cultivate; to scheme; to intend; to meditate	Panth; pathna

Por (K)	Time; period	Por (generation)
Por (R)	Feather	Par
Por	Long	Por (part)
Porab	Festival	Parab
Poran	Life	Poran
Porani	Living creature	Porani
Porbosti; parbasti (M)	To bring up; to nourish	Parwarich
Porcar	To preach	Parcar
Porcarok	A preacher	Parcarak
Porchar (M)	To preach	Parcar
Porda; parda	A curtain	Parda
Pordapos	Cherishing; care; protection	Pardapoch (being behind the curtain)
Pordhan	Chief; principal; first	Pardhan
Pordosi; pordosia	A foreigner	Pardesi
Pori (R)	Tail	Pochal
Porja	A tenant; a ryot; a subject	Parja
Porkar	Stratagem; wile; craft; cunning; kinds; sorts	Purkar (pura karegar)
Poro (M)	Blind; blindness	Poro, koro
Porokh	To recognize; to distinguish	Parakh
Porsad (M)	Food that has been offered to the deities	Parchad
Porsati; porthom	Pregnant	Garbh; ghaban
Pos; posao (+M)	Nourishing;	Pos (as in pal

	cherishing; a domesticated animal	pos; poch as generation may be a derivation)
Posan	To profit; to pay; to yield a return; to draw profit; to obtain a return	
Posan	To leak as bellows	Posan (Pb. phosi)
Poshum (R)	Wool	Poshum
Posta	The opium poppy plant	Post
Pota	Stomack	Pota
Potao	To whitewash with lime; or white earth	Poca
Potom (M)	Bundle; package	Potli
Potor; Kagoj pator	Paper; letter; documents	Patar; kagaz patar
Pototr	To strip off; to denude	Puto
Powa (M)	One-fourth seer	Powa; pa; pao
Prati (M)	Each	Parat
Pravardo (R)	Feed; nourish; provide for	Palna; parvorda
Prevta (R)	Stairs	Pori
Prosi	Neighbour	Parosi
Prya (R)	Overly; very; too many	Bharpor (Prya was a dish when sugar and ghee are put on the

		cooked rice)
Pucau	Ask	Puch
Puchal	Tail	Tail
Puche	To enquire; to ask	Puche
Puchhar (M)	To ask; asking	Puchna
Puchla	Tail	Puncch
Puchna pachni	To recognize each other	Puchna pachni
Pugri (M)	Private gain	Pugna
Puja	Worship	Puja
Pujari	A sacrificing priest; puja leader	Pujari
Pujer (K)	Distribution at a happy occasion at the birth of a child or wedding	Pujer
Pul (M)	A bridge	Pul
Pul	Bridge	Pul
Pun (+M)	Virtue; merit; religious merit	Pun
Pungi	To twist into a point	Pungi
Punji (+M)	Capita; stock	Punji
Punrrro (R)	Foot	Pair
Puphphu	Father's sister	Phuphi
Pura (+K) (+M)	Entire; complete; exact; full; perfect; total; the whole	Pura

Pura	Complete	Pura
Purab (+M)	The East	Purab
Puran	Sufficient; plenty; to fulfill; to complete; to perfect	Puran
Purana (K)	A parwana or notice	Parwana
Purana (M)	Old; ancient	Purana
Purao (M)	To complete; to fulfill; to pay in full	Purao
Purbia (+M)	Belonging to the East	Purbia
Purhut; purohit	A spiritual preceptor; Brahmans	Purohit
Puri (K)	A fairy	Pari
Puri	The world; the sea	
Puri; net puri	A contribution given towards the expenses of a funeral or marriage	Newta
Purkha (+M)	An elder; an ancestor; a patriarch	Purkha
Purus (+M)	Husband	Banda
Purus (+M) pursa	The height of a man with his and fingers	Purus

	extended above his head	
Purus	A generation	Pur; push
Pusado (R)	Penetrate; prick	Pohna
Pushel (R)	Ask; ask for; implore; request	Puchan
Pushino (R)	Invited guest	Prohna
Pushlo (R)	Invited	Puchna
Pusri (+M) pusi	A pimple	Phinsi
Pusti; Pustia	An addicted to smoking	Posti (Pb. addicted)
Pusti; pustia (+M)	A generation	Puchti
Pustik (R)	A book	Pustik
Pustok	A book	Pustok
Puthi (M)	A book	Puthi
Puthi;Kitab;Pustak	Book	Pothi;Kitab;Pustak
Putki	A nose ornament worn by women	
Putkoe	Germinate	Phutna
Putli (M)	An image	Putli
Putli; kut putri	A puppet	Putli
Putma; Putmi	Big bellied (male and female)	Patu
Pylla (K)	The pan of a pair of scales	Palla; palra
Pyrda (K)	A curtain	Parda
Pyrthei (K)	The world	Pirthawi
Pyrwa (K)	To care; to be mindful of	Parwah

	R	
Ra-na	Weeping	Rona
Raband; rubuc	Slowly; leisurely; gently	Ramke ramke
Rabhus	Ugly and lumpish	Dheus
Rabi (+M)	Cold weather Rabi crops cultivated after the secession of the rains	Rabi
Rabon raj	King Ravan	Ravan
Rabraba (M)	Of a coarse and thickly quality	Rabri
Rac	The comb of a weaver's loom	
Raca (+M)	Courtyard of a house in front	Vehra
Rad; radin	Scoundrelly; base; disobedient	Radal
Rada	A row; a line; a course; as of bricks on a wall &c.	Rada
Radi (+M)	Used up; waste; as paper; projected	Radi (Pb. Ik radi gaey ujar; Baba Farid)
Rae (+M)	Wisdom;	Rae

	opinion; counsel; order; custom	
Rae dohae	A cry out for justice	Rae dohae
Rae	Counsel	Rai
Rag (M)	Musical note; tune; air	Rag
Rag	Anger; excitement; energy; spirit	?
Raga ragi; ragar jhagar	Quarreling; disputing	Lar jhagar
Ragado (+M) Ragrao	To rub; to scrub with hands	Ragro
Ragae	Rough	?
Ragi	Spirited; active	Pb. singer
Ragra ragri	Persistently; unceasingly; fiercely as applied to quarrels or disputes	Ragra ragri
Ragrao	Friction	Ragarna
Rah	Way	Rah
Rah; raha	Road; way	Rah; raha
Rahai sahai	To shew pity; to forgive	Rahai
Rahau	To save; to deliver; to rescue	Rahau
Rahdani	Giving charity to travelers	Rahdani

Raher (M)	A kind of pulse	Arhar
Raher	A cultivated crop	Raher
Rahi	A traveler	Rahi
Rahi; rahi dandi	A kind of palki or dooli	
Rai (R)	Aristocrat; gentleman; member of the nobility	Rai
Raiyi (R)	Female rai	Rani
Raj (K) (+M)	Jurisdiction; a state; kingdom	Raj
Raj; raja (+M)	A king; a title borne by certain landlords; to reign	Raja; raja
Raj;Sarkar	Government	Raj;Sarkar
Raja;Despati	King	Raja
Rajai (M)	To reign	Rajai (hukam rajai calna NanaK); raza
Rajai	A comforter	Razai
Rajan bajan	Pomp and music	Rajan bajan
Raji (+M)	To agree; to be satisfied; to be contended	Razi
Raji nama (+M)	An acknowledgement of a cause being	Razi nama

	finally settled given by a plaintiff; a compromise	
Rajinama	Compromise	Rajinama
Rajoe; Rajosti	A kingdom	Rajwara
Rajos	Pupil of eye	?
Rakab (M)	To rise; to ascend; to lift up; to hold up	Rakab
Rakas; Rakasia (+M)	A demon	Rakhchas
Rakha (+M)	To lay an embargo on; to preserve; as a forest and game &c.	Rakh
Rakhas	A piece of wood from to 8 feet long and 6 inches broad; used to level ploughed field	Suhaga?
Rakhe (K)	To observe	Rakhi
Rakhia; rukhia	To save; relief; deliverance	Rakhia
Rakhijagao	To save; to lay by	Rakh
Rakho (K)	One who tends cattle	Rakha
Rakhwal; Rakhwar (+M)	A watchman; one who guards or watches	Rakhwala

Raksi	A machine for expressing the juice from sugar cane	Wailna
Raktao (M)	To be mad with rage	Pb. Raktan (Waris Shah)
Ralki (R)	Girl	Larki
Ram singa (M)	A long horn or pipe giving a monotonous sound	?
Ran	Medicine	Ran (used by Waris Shah)
Ran; ran bora	Pewter ; of various colors	Rang
Randhoni	A female cook	Derived from Punjabi rinana meaning cooking
Randi (+M) ranri	To become a widow; or a widower	Randi; randa
Randi	Widow	Randi
Rang-ka-tamasa (K)	A show; a display	Tamasa
Ranga (+M)	Colored; dyed	Rangia
Ranga	Colour	Rang
Rangao (M)	To color	Rangao
Rangia	Red; fair; as a person	
Rani (+M)	Queen	Rani
Rani	queen	rani
Ranjau	To persuade;	Samjau; manao

	to talk over; to beguile	
Raocao	Too much; over; applied to salting	Raocao
Raona jhaona	Weeping; crying	Raona
Ras (+M)	Juice; moisture; sap	Ras
Ras Dharia	Dance	Ras Dharia
Ras	Juice	Ras
Ras; ras jhin	Bridle; reins	Ras
Rasa	Honey; juice; sweet juice	Rasa
Rasao (M)	To tinker; to solder	Rasao
Rase rase	Slowly; leisurely	Rase rase (Rase paina; slowly adopting a path)
Rase	Soup; to prepare soup	Rase (Pb. having been trained; doing right)
Rashai (R)	Priest; clergyman	Rashi
Rashni (R)	Wife of Rashai or priestess	Rashni
Rasi (M)	Rope	Rasi
Rasi punji	Full return as in crop	Rasi punji (in which invested capital is recovered fully)
Rasia	Partner; sharer; partnership	Ralwan, Ralia
Rasiau	Lusty; applied	Rais (as rich and

	to bulls kept for breeding purpose; rich; wealthy	wealthy)
Rasid (+M)	Cor. English receipt	Rasid
Rasid	receipt	rasid
Rasik; raska (+M)	Happiness; rejoicing; pleased	
Rasta (+M)	A cart track; a road	Rasta (Pb. cart track is leeh)
Raste raste	Quietly; gently	Raste raste
Rasun (+M) rasuni	Garlic	Lasan
Rat (R)	Blood	Rat
Rat birat	During the night	Rat birat
Rat	Night	Rat
Rati	A very small quantity	Rati
Raunda	A carpenter's plane	Randa
Rawa	Temperament; disposition	Rawa (Pb. breed; as of animals)
Rawal	To lighten; to make light; light	Rawal
Rejistary; rejostora	Cor. English; Register	Rajstery
Rek; rekh	A measure of land	Rekh (line)
Res; resa risi	To copy someone; to compete in copying	Res; resa risi

Reset	Juicy; tender	Resela; rasdar
Ret rete	In line; in a row	
Ret	To come to an agreement; to conspire; to collude	Ret
Reta	To saw; as when cutting with knife; sword &c.	Reta (Pb. reti; the stone to sharpen knife sword &c. is related)
Rewaj (+M)	Season; usage; custom; fashion	Rewaj
Rihai	Liberation	Rihai
Rihai; rihat	Liberation; escape; relief; acquittal	Rehai
Rij; rijh (+M)	Choice; approbation; love; desire; wish; pleasing; satisfying	Rijh
Rijhau (+M)	To win; to persuade	Rijhau; rihjana
Rijhwar; rijhwaria (+M) rijhua	Merry; lighthearted	Rijhia; rijhau
Rin (+M) rinrni	Debt; to borrow	Rin (Pb. Rin is cooking also)
Ringsur (K)	To sing	Rag gawna
Ris risi (M)	Ruffled	Ris risi
Rish (R)	Bear	Rich

Rishari (R)	Man who works with preforming bears	Madari
Rishni (R)	Female bear	Richni
Rit; ritu	Season; custom; habit to	Rit; rut season)
Ritha (M)	A kind of tree; the fruit of which is used as a substitute for soap to cleanse the cloths	Retha
Riti (K)	Established customs	Riti
Roa (M)	Transplant	Roa (Pb. nasal; of the generation)
Roco	To seize the top with tips of the fingers	Noco
Rod (M)	To cancel	Rad
Rog	Defect	Rog
Rog; Roga; rugi (+M)	Disease; illness; defect; infirmity; disorder; malady	Rog; rugi (who has rog)
Rohni; ruhni	A period of 13 days beginning on the 13th of Jeth	Rauni (preparation for sowing)
Rohr (M)	To dry; to	Ror (by roasting)

	become emaciated	
Roj (+M)	Daily	Roz
Rojgar	Livelihood	Rujgar
Rojgar; rojaria (+M)	To earn; to earn daily; earner	Rojgar; rojgaria
Rok; rokao (+M)	To stop; to prevent; to prohibit	Rokao
Roka	Ready money; cash	Rok; Rokra
Rokot (+M)	Blood	Rakat
Roktok (+M)	Obstruction; impediment; to raise objections or difficulties	Roktok
Roktok	objections	Roktok
Rond khond; ronkhond (+M)	To discuss; to debate; to talk over	Rond khond (Pb. rond marna means to use unjust tricks in game or playing
Rong (K)	Color; paint; a show; a display	Rang
Rosao	To be absorbed in; to be engrossed in	Rasao
Rosod; rasad	Provision for travelers	Rasad
Roti	Bread	Roti
Rovel (R)	Cry; shed tears; weep	Rovan

Rudi	Waste; rejected	Radi
Rui (+K)	Cotton	Rui
Rui rui	Rapidly	
Rui;Kapsara	Cotton	Roon; Kapah
Ruji (M)	Female organ of generation	
Ruk	Trees	Rukh
Rukar; rukhar	Dry	Rakar
Rukh (R)	Tree	Rukh
Rumar	A pocket handkerchief	Rumal
Rup (R)	Silver	Rupa
Rup	Form; appearance	Rup
Rupa (+K)	Silver	Rupa
Rusa rusi (+M)	Not to be on speaking terms	Rusa rusi
Ruti (K)	A loaf; bread	Roti
Ryat (R)	Night	Rat
Rynsun	Garlic	Lasan
	S	
Sa (M)	Side; edge; season	Sa
Sa (R)	All; everybody	Sare
Sa-ar (M)	Arrow	Sa-ar (ar is something that can penetrate; ploughmen or cartmen fix a nail at the end of stick to move bullocks)
Sa-de-yakh	All of a	Ik-dam

	sudden	
Sa-vaxt (R)	All the time; always	Har-vakt
Sab (K)	Cleanly	Saph
Sabab (+M)	Reason; cause; motive; accusation; on account of; by reason of	Sabab
Sabad (+M)	Sound; noise; voice	Shabad (Pb. words)
Sabah	Spur	Sabah (Pb. mannerism; temperament)
Sabasi	Distinction; celebrity; fame; glory	Shabashi
Sabbo;Harek	Every	Sab;Harek
Sabha (+M)	Council; an assembly convened for consultations; deliberations and settlement of disputed matters	Sabha
Sabiah (K)	All	Sabha
Sabik	Original; former	Sabik
Sabit (+M)	To be perfect; to be complete; excellent;	Sabit

	proved	
Sabja; sabjao	To become moist by attracting moisture	Sabja (grass or greenery)
Sabol	Crowbar	Sabal
Sabon (K)	Soap	Sabun
Sabud	To prove	Sabut
Sabur; sabri (+M)	To wait; have patience	Sabir
Sabut (K)	Proof	Sabut
Sabut (M)	Proof	Sabut
Sac (+M) saca	A mould	Saca
Sacai	Truthfulness; honesty	Sacai
Sad	Sound; to sound	Sad
Sad; sadh	Wish; desire; inclination	Sadh (Pb. sadhar)
Sadae; sadai (M)	Continually; daily; always; forever	Sada
Sadagar (M)	A trader; especially a cloth merchant	Sudagar
Sadamod; Sadamad	Continuously; without a break	Sadain (shadomad means fiercely)
Saddi; sadhi	Strength; ability; power	Siddi; sirar
Sadhao	To train; to discipline	Sadhao
Sadharan (M)	Common	Sadharan
Sadharon	Common; common	Sadharon

	place	
Sadhin	Independent; free; one's own master	Sadhin; sirri
Sadhu	A medicant; a fakir	Sadhu
Sadhu; sarhu	Relationship between the husbands of sisters	Sandu
Sae (+M)	A hundred	Sae; sao
Saekra	Per hundred; percent	Saekra
Saetan (M)	Devil; Satan	Chetan
Sagai (M)	A form of marriage of widows	
Sagai	Relationship; kinship	Sagai (engagement)
Sagak	The awns of certain grasses	Sagak (Sag)
Sagam (M)	Turnip	Chaljam; gonglo
Sagen; sangen (M)	To bud; to sprout	Sag
Sagu dana (M)	Sago	Sagu dana
Sagun (M)	Good omen	Shagun
Sagun	omen	sagan
Sah; sa	Side; edge	Saha
Sahae (M)	Help; assistance	Sahae
Sahaj	Easy	Sahaj
Sahaj; sahoj; sohoj (+M)	Easy; light	Sahaj
Sahao (+M)	To suffer; to bear; to endure; to	Sahna

	put up with; to be patient	
Sahao	Endurance	Sahna
Sahas	Courage	Sahas
Saheb (+M)	A European	Saheb; sab
Saher (M) sahar	A town	Shaher
Sahet	To breath	Sah lena
Sahi (M)	Witness	Sahi
Sahi	To favor; friendly	Sahi; hami
Sahta; sasta	Cheap; low; as a rate or price	Sasta
Saiman;somon	similar	saman
Saj	Decorate	Saj
Sajai (+K) Saja (+M) sajai	To punish; to deal retributive justice	Saza
Sajao (+M)	To adorn; to harness; to put in; fill in; to cloth	Sajao
Sajao	To be seemingly; befitting; proper; becoming	Sajhao; sajaia
Sajbaj	Equipment; implements; harness; tools; materials; machinery	Sajbaj (conspiracy)
Sajha (+M)	Together; in common; in	Sajha; sanjha

	partnership	
Sajha	Common	Sanjha
Sak	Vegetable	Sag
Saka (+M)	The relationship between family	Sak (relatives)
Sakar	Partially refined sugar	Shakar
Sakarkenda (+M) shakarkanda	The sweet potatoes	Sakarkandi
Sakarkenda	sweet potato	sakarkenda
Sakat (M)	Hard; strong	Sakhat
Sakha (M)	Conch shell bangle	Sankh
Sakhi (+K) (+M)	A witness; a token; in earthwork a â€œbenchmarkâ€.	Sakhi; shahaditi; gawah
Sakhi (M)	To make friends between the persons of the same name; friend; a companion	Sakhi; sahali
Sakim	To finish; to complete	Khatam
Sakit	To congeal; to become dense	Sakit (motionless)
Sakor (K)	Unrefined sugar	Shakar
Sakra	Narrow; strait; not	Sukra

	being room enough	
Sakti; sokti; sukti	Strength; power; ability	Shakti
Sal	Year	Sal
Sala (M)	Brother-in-law	Sala
Sala +M) salah	To pick out impurities;	Salah
Salami (+M)	A present given to a landlord for granting a lease or bestowing a favor; a present given to a superior	Salami (Pb. money or gift given on a wedding)
Salat; galat salat	Stupid; dull witted	Galat salat
Salavari (R)	Bridle; rein	Savari
Sale sale	In season; at the proper time	Sale sale
Salgao (M)	To kindle; to lit up	Salgao
Salha; solho	To advise; to consult; to be in harmony	Salah
Salis; salisdar	To mediate; an arbitrator	Salis
Salsi (M)	To arbitrate	Salsi
Salu	Red cotton cloth	Salu
Saman (+M)	Equal; similar; alike;	Saman

	akin; the same	
Saman	Front	Samane
Saman. Somon; (+M)	Cor. English summon	saman
Saman; samna samni (+M) samang	Front; to front or face	Samna; samne
Samanom	An obsolete name for gold	
Samao (+M)	To be contained in	Samao; samana
Samaro (M)	To manage; to conduct ably	Sanwaro
Sambhob	Possible; probable	Sambho
Sambound	Affinity	Sambandh
Sambrao; sambhrao (+M)	To hold or keep together; to sustain; to assist; to help	Sambhalo
Samdhi (+M)	Father-in-laws	Samdhi; kuram
Samet; samit	With; along with; together with	Samait
Samjhao (+M)	To comprehend; to understand; to explain; to convince; warn; persuade	Samjhao

Samjhao	Admonish	Samjhana
Sampak sampok	Relationship	sak
Samporon (M)	To be ready; ready	Samporon
Samtao	To constringe; to compress; to collect; to amass; to fold up	Samtao; samatina
Samuchi (R)	Almost; nearly	Samuci
Samud; samut; samundar; samundar (+M)	The sea	Samundar
Samuk	In front of	Samuk
Samun	To end; to finish	samuna
San (R)	You are	Sain
San bhai (+M) sang bhai	A companion	
San	A revolving whetstone used for sharpening razors; knives &c.	San
Sanak	Instantly; at once	Achanak
Sanam	All	Sare
Sanang (M)	Wish; desire; intention	Tahaang
Sanc	A mould	Saca
Sand (+M) sandi	A bull	Sand (Pb. sanda is male buffalo)
Sand	Bull	Sanh
Sang (K)	Forbidden;	Sang (shame)

	taboo	
Sanga (+M) sang	A friend; a companion; a comrade	Sangi
Sanga (M)	Pith of a plant; thick round root of a plant	Sanga
Sanga	A beam laid breadthwise supporting the roof of a house	Shahtir
Sangar (M)	To hunt	Chakar
Sangat (M)	A wooden pole	Sangat
Sangin	A bayonet	Sangin
Sangut	Used by brothers-in-laws when addressing each other	Sangat (A gathering; a froup)
Sani (+M)	Over; again	Sani (second)
Sanj (M)	Half a day	Sanj (evening)
Sanjau	To be determined; to have made up one's mind; to be prepared; to be angry; to be excited; to rouse anger	Sanjau
Sanjholi	Evening	Sanjh
Sanjohi	Evening; beginning at evening and	Sanjh; sanjh

	lasting long	
Sanjok (+M) sanjog	Opportunity; proper time; timely	Sanjog
Sank	A conch	Sankh
Sankha (M)	Branch; family branch	Chakh
Sansan (+M) sansoon	Silent; hushed; no sound audible	Sansan
Sansanao	To be excited or frenzied	Sansanao
Sansar; sonsar	The world	Sansar
Santali	English	Punjabi
Santap	Affliction; distress	Santap
Santhi maric	A kind of pepper	Mirac
Santi	peace	santi
Sanwar	A companion	Sanwaria
Sao	Together; with; along with	Sao
Saoar (M)	A rider	Sawar
Saoda; soeda (+M)	Trade; traffic; marketing; wares; merchandise; goods; to trade; to traffic; to buy; to purchase	Soda
Saoha	Well; befitting;	Soha, sohanda

	proper; seemly	
Saora; sauri	Dark grey color (male and female)	Sanwra; sanwala; sanwri; sanwali
Sap (R)	Snake	Sap
Sapaharia	A snake charmer	Sapera
Sapha(+M)	Clean; clear; distinct	Saph
Saphai (+M)	To settle a dispute; to clear up a disputed matter	Saphai
Saphar (+M)	A journey; a tour	Saphar
Saphor	Tour	Safar
Sapno (R)	Like a snake; vicious; vindictive	Sap-har
Saport; soport; sapurd; supurd (+M)	To make over to; to give in custody; to entrust; to deliver	Supurd
Sapot	Gentle; quite; peaceable; pacific	Sapot (Pb. brave; good son)
Saprum	Completely; fully; entirely	Salam
Sar (K)	A Kashmiri chadar	Shal
Sar (R)	According to; as; as far as; as much as;	Sar

	how; like; resembling	
Sar o pai	Easily; fluently; like water	Pani-sar
Sar sagun	Sagun wood	Sagon
Sar	Level; smooth	Sar (iksar; on one level)
Sar-mothon (R)	As they say	Ohnan-sar
Sara	A funeral pyre	Sara
Sarae	A series of sticksfixed in the ground upon which a weaver sets his wrap	Sarae
Sarai	A caravanserai; a native inn	Sarai
Saranga (+m) Sarangi	A kind of a fiddle	Sarangi
Sarap	Curse	Sarap
Sarapia	A curser; one given to cursing	Sarapia (siapa)
Sarasar	Equally; not inferior or superior to each other; neck to neck	Sarasar
Sarbat	sherbet	sharbat
Sarbat; sarbot	Sherbet	Sharbat
Sarbharao; sorbhorao	To have presence of mind; to	Sarbharao (leader)

	occur to one on the spur of the moment	
Sardar (+M)	A foreman; chief or headman	Sardar (chief; head of a tribe)
Sardar	Foreman	Sardar
Sardi	To be at the maximum; utmost; to be in full swing	Sardi (to what one can do)
Sare-la-lumyako (R)	Belonging to the whole world	Sansarak
Sarekai (R)	Everywhere	Sab-than
Sarhad; sohod (+M)	A boundary	Sarhad
Sarhad;Sima	Boundary	Sarhad;Sima
Sarhar	Long; straight and with few knots; as timber	Sarhar
Sari (R)	To make; to create	Usarna
Sari	True; to take in earnest	Sari
Sarik; sarikdar	A partner; a shareholder	Sharik; sharakat dar
Sarishta	Applied mainly to the office in which the court records are kept; the records of a court	Sarishta

Sarishtadar	Keeper of court records	Sarishtadar
Sarkar; sorkar (+M)	The government; teacher of a village school	Sarkar
Sarkari (+M)	Belonging to a state or government	Sarkari
Sarlaba (M)	Rotten; used contemptuously	Saria busia
Sarlak	A splinter of a wood	Shilar
Sarota (+M)	A knife used to cut the arcca nuts	Sarota (knife to cut Shalia)
Sarpat	To finish	Sarpat (immediately)
Sarpharia	Clever; quick-witted; handy; adroit; applied to young person	Sarphira
Sarti (M)	True; truth	Sarti
Sas (R)	There was	Si
Sasan (M)	Burial ground	Chamchan
Sasang (M)	Turmeric	Haldi
Sasrar	Father-in-law's house	Sasral; sohre
Sasta (M)	Cheap	Sasta
Sasta	Cheap	Sasta
Sasto (R)	Healthy; well; intact; perfect;	Salam; sabat

	having no defect; sound; sturdy	
Sastor	scriptures	sastar
Sastro (R)	Father-in-law	Sohra; susar
Sasuriar (M)	In-laws house	Susral; sohre
Sat (+M) sarti	True; truth; evidence	Sat
Sat marte	Immediately	Sat marde
Sat	Truth	Sat
Sata	On account of; in lieu of	Sata (like in wata sata)
Satahi	Seven days rain; heavy continuous rain	
Satao (+M)	To put close together; to stick together	Satao
Satao (M)	To persecute; to give trouble	Satao; sata
Sate	Eaves; the extent of roof projecting over the walls	Shat
Sati	To be burned alive with husband	Sati
Satia (K)	To feel annoyed at	Satia; sataia
Satpat (M)	Quickly	Satpat; sarpar
Satru	An enemy	Shatru
Satu (+M)	Meal; flour	Satu (flour from near ripened

		grain)
Sau (M)	A money lender	Sau; chahukar
Sauti	A companion	Sathi
Sava (R)	All; everything	Sara
Saw; Sywa (K)	To put near the fire; to expose to the action of smoke	Pb. Sawa (ashes)
Sawa (+M)	One fourth more	Sawa
Sawad (M)	Taste; tasteful	Sawad
Sawai (M)	Interest at 25%	Sawai
Sawal (+M)	A question	Sawal
Sawal	question	sawal
Sawalia	A speaker; one able to address a court or panchayat &c.	Relating to question
Sawang (M)	Strength	Sawang (to pose as someone else)
Se	That; that same	Se
Sea	To rot; to decompose	Sarna; galna
Sean (+M)	Adult; well grown; cunning; crafty; sharp; artful	Seana

Sebot	Proof; without doubt	Sebot
Sedae	Long time ago; ancient time	Sedae
Sehoe	The same; the like	Sehoe
Sekao	To apply heat; to foment	Sekao
Seke seke	To rageo fumee;	Tap; tap cana
Sekra (M)	Soon; quick	Cheti
Semana (R)	Seed; sperm; pollen	
Semesto (R)	People; family; relations	Sak
Sen	Direction; side; quarter; towards	Sen (line; make lines by plough or other implements)
Senra (M)	Wise; intelligent	Siana
Ser (+M)	Seer=80 tola; about Â½ lbs	Sair; ser
Serec	To snivel; to have a discharge from the nose; eyes or mouth	Chanana
Seta (M)	Early morning ; 7 AM	Swele
Sewa; sewa dowa; sewa	To worship;	Sewa

tewa	to serve	
Shah (K)	To suffer; to endure	Sahna
Shaiti (K)	A letter	Chithi
Shakhait (K)	To handle or deal severely; to gnaw	Sakhti
Shalai (K)	To manage	Chalai
Shalak (K)	Clever; active; tactful	Chalak
Shalvarya (R)	Harem pants; ankle length puffy pants worn by Muslim Romani women	Chalvar
Shara (K)	Small shot	Shara
Sharak (K)	A lamp	Charag
Shata (K)	An umbrella	Shata; shatri
Sheyorri (R)	Pre-adolescent girl	Chuhri
Shib (R)	Tongue; language; speech	Jib
Shing (R)	Antler; horn	Sing
Shir-ryn-ieng (K)	From head to foot	Sharir (Full body)
Shisha (K)	True; real; indeed; of course	Shisha (Pb. when used as verb ; sisha hu gia)
Shlim (K)	A small earthen cup fitted to a hookah for	Cilim

	smoking	
Shlor (K)	Brave; courageous; daring	Daler
Shogora (R)	Wife's sister; sister-in-law	Sali
Shoh (K)	Pleasing; touching; affecting	Shoh (Pb. shoh as beloved)
Shon (R)	Moon	Chun
Shornango (R)	Bareheaded	Nange-sir
Shosha (R)	Rabbit	Seha; seyar
Shoshni (R)	Female rabbit	Sehi
Shtar (R)	Four	Car
Shuri (R)	Kitchen knife	Churi
Shutak (K)	1/16 of a seer	Chatank
Si (R)	To be	Si
Si kai (R)	There is/are about/around	Sane
Si	To plough	Sian is derivation
Siahi (+M)	Ink	Siahi
Sian; sianti (K)	Clever; intelligent	Sian; siana
Siaw (K)	A whistle	Seti
Sid	Effected; accomplished; perfected	Sudh
Sidari;Maliki	Authority	Sirdari
Sidbid	Accomplished; finished; settled	Sidbid (sudh budh; to be aware of; to know somewhat
Sidha	Straight	Sidha
Sidho	Clean; perfect	Sidho

Sieng (K)	Smelling like snuff or chillies	Sungna
Sig; signo; sigo	Shortly; soon; quickly	Cheti
Sihat	Bees' wax	Shahad
Siikar	To confess; to acknowledge	Suikar
Sik; sikte	Mode; way; method	Sik; saidh (Pb. sik means pain of separation; yearning)
Sika	A small silver coin; or coin	Sika
Sikari; sikria	A hunter	Shikari
Sikat; sikhat; sikhan	Teaching	Sikhan
Sikavel (R)	Advise; educate; guide; teach	Sikhawan
Sikha	A small iron rod to clean the hooka	Sikha (used for roasting kababs)
Sikhansu	Educate	Sikhna
Sikhao (M)	To teach; to tutor	Sikhao
Sikhat	Teaching	Sikhya
Siki;Sika	Coin	Sika
Sikil	To polish; to burnish; to make bright as iron on a grindstone	Sikil
Sikir	Itching; burning; dislike; antipathy;	Sikir (head sikri is from this root)

	hate	
Sil	A hone; to rub and sharpen on a hone	Sil
Silat; silot; silau (+M)	A slate; a school slate	Silat
Sili	A rope made of hair	Saili
Silpher; silphera	To change from civility to craziness	Sirphira
Sima (+M) simana	Boundary	Sima
Sima	Limit	Sima
Sind kati	The implement by which thieves make hole in the wall	Sanh kati
Sind muhani	The act of making a hole in the wall for breaking in	
Sind; sindh	To break into a house by making a hole in the wall	Sanh
Sindan	Mischief making	Sanhan
Sinduk	A box; a chest	Sinduk
Sindur bundi	Marked with sindur	Sindur bindi
Sinduri (M)	Vermilion	Sanduri
Sing (K)	A lion	Singh; sheenh

Sing	Horn	Sing
Singa; ram singa	A ram's horn; a musical instrument shaped like a buffalo horn	Sing (horn of any animal)
Singar (+M)	To bath and tidy oneself; to adorn	Singar
Singar	Nightfall; the period following the twilight	
Singhason	A throne	Singhason
Sini (R)	Tray	Sini
Sipahi (M)	Policeman	Sipahi
Sir (R)	Garlic	Lasan
Sir panch	Headman of a â€˜panch]	Sirpanc
Sir soro	Flowing; as blood or water from a small opening	Sir (naksir is sir from noose)
Sirba	To have a splinter run into the hand	Shilat
Sirhi	Ladder	Sirhi
Siri (+M) sirhi	A ladder; a stair	Siri; pauri
Siri	To enquire; to search; to look out for	Siri; sira labhna
Sirini (M)	Offering	Chirini
Sirir	Dew	Tarail
Sirjan; sirjon (+M)	To create; to begin; to	Sijan; sirjana

	prepare	
Siropa	Two sticks tied together to prop up the cart when the bullocks are unyoked.	Sonka
Siropa; siripa	A piece of cloth ; generally suitable for a turban given as as a sign of office or authority or as respect	Siropa
Sirpuc	A piece of male attire used to cover the head	Sirpuch
Sis	An ear of dhan	Sis (head)
Sisa (+M)	Lead	Sisa
Sisi sisi; siu	To whistle through the teeth	Siti
Sisi	Whistle	Siti
Siswa bajra	A kind of cultivated grain	Bajra
Sitar	A kind of guitar	Sitar
Sito	To become cold	Seet
Siu (M)	To plough	Siu
Skeri (R)	Ladder; stairway	Siri; pori

Skhem (K)	Firm; firmly; securely	Sakhat
Skoc	To shog; to shake upto toss	Skoc
Skopil (R)	Castrate; geld; make impotent	Khasi
Smai(K)	To swear; take an oath	Sonh
So	Hundred	So
Soan (M)	To smell	Sungna
Soba	To pierce something thicker than a needle or thorn	Soa
Sobbo kal	All time; any time	Sabho kal; har wele
Sobbo	All; every	Sabho
Sobha	To adorn; pleasant; beautiful	Shobha
Sobhab; sobhaw	Nature; disposition; temperament	Sobhao; sobha
Sobori	Patient; enduring	Sabar
Soc	To consider; to think over; thought	Soc
Sod	Interest	Sod; biaj
Sod; sodh	To clear; to liquidate	Sodh (to clean up as writings &c.)
Sodae	Every day;	Sada

	always	
Sodo	Sound produced by water falling into water	Soda
Soetan	Satan; the devil	Shetan
Soghor; sughor	Well behaved	Sughar
Sohag	Deference; affability; love; dear	Sohag
Sohan; sohar; sohara	Beautiful; charming; pleasant	Sohan; sohna
Sohan; sohna	Susceptible to injury; easily killed; lacking vitality	Sohal
Sohda (M)	Disobedient	Chohda
Sohij; sohboj	Easy; light	Sahaj
Sohja; sahje (+M) sojh	Straight; upright; without duplicity; simple	Sidha
Sokhao; sokhat	To dry up; to become parched;	Sokhao
Sokol; sengel sokol	Fire	
Sokor	Applied to gurgling sound in the throat	Shokar
Sokto	Hard; tight	Sakhat
Sol saluki; sola saluk	Peace;	Sulah saluk

	harmony	
Solah; soloh	To advise; to consult	To consult; to be in harmony
Som (+M) somwar	Monday	Somwar; sanwar
Somani	Many; much; great	Samani (be-saro-samani is opposite)
Somband	Connection; affinity; relation	Sambandh
Sombond	Connection	Sambandh
Somo (R)	Just; now only	Saman
Somoe	Time	Saman; same
Somojos	Equally; justly; in equal parts	Ik-jor
Sompot	Moveable Property	Sampat
Son	The fiber yielding plant	Son
Son; songe (+M)	In company of; along with	Sang
Sona (+M)	Gold	Sona
Sonar (M)	Goldsmith	Sonar
Sonat	Circumcision	Sontan
Sondgond	Fragrant ; as a smell; perfume; aroma	Sogand
Sondhar	Pleasant	Shandar
Sonhar	A goldsmith	Sonar; soniara
Sonjog (M)	By chance; seldom	Sanjog
Sonori (R)	Sound	Sunan
Sonth (M)	Dry ginger	Sonth

Sontor	To be careful; vigilant; careful; alert; prudent; watchful; heedful	Sawadhan
Sontori	A military guard	Santri
Sor (K)	A station; an enlightened town	Shehar
Sordar (K)	A village headman	Sardar
Sordol	A piece of timber laid along the the top of a wall on which rests the beams which supports a ceiling ; or the floor of an upper story	Sardal
Sorma surmi (+M) sarom	To put to shame	Sharminda
Sormi; be-sormi	Shameless	Be-sharmi
Sormia	Modest; shamefaced	Sharmila
Sorom	shame	sharam
Soron soron	Suffering from a bad cold; who is snuffling	Son Son
Soros	To be superior to;	Sorma

	in size; skill; wisdom; strength ; speed &c.	
Sorpha	Cheap; Abundant	Sarpha (To save; to spend carefully)
Sorr; sorro (R)	All; every; the whole	Saro
Sorro-ryato (R)	All night	Sari rat
Soso	Breathing	Sah
Sostor	Scriptures; sacred books	Shastar
Sot	True; truth; evidence or assurance	Sat
Sota (M)	A stick	Sota
Soto (M)	To place in proper order	Soto
Sovel (R)	Sleep; be sleep	Savan; .sSona
Stet (K)	Fast; quickly	Jhat
Suba	A military leader	Suba
Subha; subhab	Suspicion	Shuba
Subita	Well; excellent; opportune; convenient; satisfaction	Subota
Suca; such	Truthful (male and female)	Suca; suci
Sud (M)	Interest	Sud
Sudakur ; bydakor (K)	A merchant	Sudagur
Sudh	Cleanse	Shudh

Sudh; Thik Thak	Accurate	Thik Thak
Sudh; sudho	Pure; unpolluted; accurate	Sudh
Sudha; sudhao	To pet or sooth by stroking or rubbing; as cat; horse; bullock &c.	Sudha
Sudha; sudhau	The whole; along with	Pura, sudhia hoia
Sudhar; Sudhrau; Sudrau (+M) sudhar	To repair; to put to rights; to mend	Sudhar
Sudhe	Empty; only	Shudhi
Sudhet	To calm a restive cow by patting	
Sudu (K)	A fool; a simpleton	Sidha
Sui (+M)	Needle	Sui
Sui	Needle	Sui
Suj; suj buj (+M)	Understanding; reasoning power; power of comprehension	Suj; suj buj
Sujhan	To see; to see anything particularly	Sujhan; sian
Suk	Ease; tranquility; content; happiness	Sukh

Sukau	Dry	Sukka
Sukhal (M)	Dried	Suki
Sukhi; sukhwar; sukwar (+M) suku	Accustomed to ease; brought up in comfortable circumstances	Sukhi
Sukowar (M) sukraur	Friday	Shukarwar
Sukraj	In comfort; at ease; ease loving	Sukhraj
Sukrtol (R)	Make shorter; shortness	Sukrna
Sukulbar	Friday	Shukarbar
Sul (M) sul	Dysentry; any griping pain	Sul (Pb. extreme stomach pain; long thorn)
Sulakh	A long thatching needle; a kind of hairpin	Sulakh (an iron bar)
Sulgao (+M)	To kindle; to light; to cause to burn; to inflame	Sulgao
Sulta	A piece of rag twisted to make a lamp wick	Sulta
Suluc (+M) sulni	Snot; mucus discharged from the noose	Seendh

Suluk	Peace; harmony	Suluk
Sum	Miserly; niggardly; parsimonious	Sum; soom (a miser)
Suman	To become quiet; to come out and leave as a spirit which had possessed one	Suman
Sun; suna; sunsan (+M)	Empty; desolate	Sun (struck as wonderment; deserted; loose sensation of a body part due to keeping it stationary)
Sunan	Hear	Sunn
Sunan; Sunani	To cause to hear; to tell; to inform; to hear; to listen to; to have effect; as medicine	Sunan; sunani
Sund	Trunk Elephants	Sund
Sundar mukhi	Good looking	Sundar mukhi
Sundar; sundor (+M)	Beautiful; pretty	Sundar
Sung (R)	Aroma; odor; smell	Sung
Suno (R)	Dream	Suphna
Sunr (M)	Trunk of an	Sund

	elephant	
Sur (K)	Tune; voice; sound	Sur
Surag		
Surahi (+M)	A porous earthenware water bottle	Surahi
Suraj mukhi	The sun flower	Suraj mukhi
Suraj; suruj	The sun	Suraj
Surhi	A kind of weevil which infests stored dhan	Susri
Surkau	To sniff; to suck up	Surkna
Surma; surman	To be excited; to be frenzied; fury; desperation; impatience	Surma (Pb. brave)
Surok (K)	A road	Sarak
Susti (+M)	Laziness; slow; idle	Susti
Susu	To sniff; to snort	Susu
Sut (K)	Interest	Sod
Sut	To dress or tie up hair	Sut
Sutam	Yarn	Sut
Suto (R)	Sleep	Suto
Suv (R)	Needle	Sui
Suvel (R)	Embroider	
Suvimos (R)	Embroidery	
Suvyako kan (R)	Eye of the	Sui da kan

	needle	
Suwaga (K)	Borax	Suhaga
Suwan (K)	Satisfied; complete	Suwaia hona
Swadhin	Independent	Swadhin
Swagdar (R)	Always; all the time	Sada
Syrngiew (K)	A shadow	Saya; parchawan
	T	
Tabe	Dependent; subject	Tabe
Tabe-do (M)	Than; after than; subsequently	Tadon
Tabedar (+M)	A dependent; a follower	Tabedar
Tabedar	Follower	Tabedar
Taber (M)	To bend forward	Tabar
Tabij	An ornament worn on the upper arm	Taweez
Tabla (+K)	A small drum beaten with the fingers; a small hatchet or axe	Tabla
Tablo (R)	Warm up	Tap
Tad-ynda (K)	Until; till; when	Tad; tadon
Tada; tunda	To touch lightly with point of anything; a stick; the	Thunga

	finger &c.	
Tadbir; tatbir (+M)	To deliberate; to take counsel; opinion or advice; to make necessary enquiries	Tadbir
Taeom; taiom (M)	After; following; back; behind	Taeon
Tagada (+M)	To insist upon a thing being done at once; to cause to do quickly	Takaza
Tagar	A trough	Tagar
Tagot (M)	Strength	Takat
Taha	Certainly; without doubt	Intaha
Taha; jaha taha	In some places	Jithe kite
Tahao; tahaote	Feeling the way; groping as with a stick to try the depth of water; or in darkness	Tahao (from teh)
Tahas; tahas nahas	To waste; to squander	Tahas; tahas nahas (to destroy)
Tahi	That; that same	Tahi; tahin

Tahrao (M)	To fix; to settle; come to a decision or dtermination; to appoint; to establish; to stop; to stay; to remain; to be permanent	Thahrao
Tahsil; tasil (M)	To collect dues	Tahsil
Tahsildar (M)	Collector of dues	Tahsildar
Taikena (M)	Was; used; was in habit of	Takia (takia karna)
Tain (M)	To stay; to remain	Athain; tikna
Tair (K) (+M)	To get ready; to prepare	Tiar
Taj; Taja (M)	Fresh; fat; green	Taza
Tajbij (M)	Consideration; judgement; opinion; consider	Tajwez
Tajia	Shia ensemble	Taazia
Tak	Double once without cutting	Tak
Taka (+M)	Silver; a rupee; money	Taka

Takao	To look at; to watch; to look intently	Takao; takna
Takda (K)	Urgent	Takid
Takh (R)	Armpit	Kach
Takhuh ; tynkhuh (K)	To knock the head against	Takkar
Takia (+M)	A pillow	Takia; sarahana
Takic	To meet with an obstacle; difficulty; or hindrance	Atkal; daka
Takoe	To spin on the charkha or spinning wheel	Takoe
Takonia	Staring; stare	Takna; tak
Takra tukra	Pieces; fragments; broken	Takra; tukra (Dakra means big piece)
Takra tukro (M)	A broken piece	Tukra
Takrar (M)	To dispute; to jangle; to argue; to wrangle; to quarrel	Takrar
Takrar	Argue	Takrar
Takta (+M)	A plank; a board	Takhta
Takta	Board	Takhta
Taktaki	Stockstill; startled; and deprived of power of motion	Tinktiki

Taku	The spinning axle of a spinning wheel on which the thread is wound as it spins	Takla
Tal	Equal without change; musical time or measure	Tal
Tala (+K) (+M)	A lock; a padlock	Tala; jindra
Tala	Middle; center	Tala (water pool as well)
Talab (M)	Wages	Talab
Talao (M)	A tank of water	Tala
Talao	To spend or pass as time	Talao (to postpone)
Talasi (K)	To search	Talachi
Talbi	To hurry; to act without delay; promptly; quickly	Talbi (to ask someone to present him/herself)
Taletal	Without intermission; continuously	Chalochal
Talha	A short stick used to throw at small game; or to knock down fruit	Tahanga
Talim	To tesach; to	Talim

	instruct	
Talka (M)	The palm of the hand. Sole of the foot	Tali; tala
Talmalao		
Taloi (R)	Palate; roof of the mouth	Talo
Taltalao	To cause to haste; to hurry; to dragoon	Calcalao
Taluk	A lease in perpetuity; a subdivision of a zila	Taulak; taulka
Talukdar	A landlord; holder or proprietor of a taluk	Taulakdar
Talukdari	The tenure; office or state of a Talukdar	Talukdari
Tam (+M)	Thine; your	Tam; tuhada
Tam (K)	To pick up; to gather	Tam jam
Tam-tamao (M)	To be in readiness	
Tam; tham (M)	To beat	Tunbna (tamaca seems derivation)
Tamakhur; thamakhur (+M) tamskhu	Tobacco	Tmaku; tambaku
Tamao. tamtamao	To be enraged; to be excited	Tapao

	with anger	
Tamasa (+M)	An entertainment; a spectacle; a show	Tamasha
Tamasuk; tomosuk (+M)	A note of hand; bond; obligation	Tamasuk
Tamba (M)	Copper	Tamba
Tambu (+M)	A tent	Tambu
Tambura (R)	A musical instrument	Tambura
Tamil (+M)	To put in force; d decree; to take possession of; to be in charge; to appoint	Tamil
Tamuti (M)	Untrained; inexperienced	Tamak toi
Tan	To be scarce; to be insufficient; dearth	Tan
Tanabhana (+M)	To make preparations to begin a work; inner details	Tanabana
Tanao	To draw out; to stretch; to drag; to be drawn	Tanao
Tanatani	To be at	Tanatani

	loggerheads; to be at variance; to contend; to be at strife; to pull at each other	
Tanda (+M)	To straddle; to keep the legs far apart from each other	Tanda (a separate standing plant)
Tandha; thandha	Cold; chill; comforted ; pacified	Thanda
Tandha;Thandha	Cold	Thanda
Tang (R)	Confined; tight; narrow	Tang
Tangao	To hang up; to suspend	Tangao
Tangi (+M)	To wait for; tarry for	Tahngi
Tangna	A peg; or anything on which anything is hung or placed	Tangna
Tani (M)	Is he ?	Taion; weaving
Tantanao	To tighten by pulling or stretching; as a rope &c.	Tantanao
Tanti (M)	A weaver	Tanti
Tao	To heat; to be heated; to be excited; to	Tao; ta

	heat to a white heat as iron	
Tapam	To wrestle	Tapna
Tapan	To be scarce; to be insufficient; dearth	Tapan (to pass difficult time when things are scarce or difficult)
Tapar; tuar tapar	Orphans; orphand	Tapar
Taphim	To recognize; to know	Taph-him
Tapi	To deceive	Tapi
Tapis	Force; energy; violence; vehemence; rage; fury	Tapash
Tapra topra (M)	Small	Tapar
Taptapa	Wide apart; wide spread; sprawling	Taptapa
Tapu (+M)	An island; to overflow or flood as water	Tapu
Tar (+M)	Wire; the telegraph	Tar
Tar (K)	To tear; to rend	Tartar
Tar	Proper way or method	Tar
Tara tari	To hurry; to do quickly	Tara tari
Tarajur (K)	Scales;	Tarazo; takri

	balance	
Taram	To step; a step	Kadam
Taran (M)	Shoulder	Taran (Pb. utmost strength)
Tarao	To deflect; to turn aside; to remove by pushing away or drawing towards	Khiskao
Tarbhuj; tarbuj; tarmuj	The sweet melon; watermelon	Tarbuz; hadwana
Tarch; tarchao; tircha; tirchau	Slanting; at an angle; obliquely slop; curve; off the straight	Tircha
Tari turi	Below; down; underneath; under; over the top	Tari (a swimming lap)
Tari	Liquor made from the juice of the toddy palm	Tari
Tarik; tarikh (+K) (+M)	Date; date of the month	Tarikh
Tarjama	Translate	Tarjama
Tarjuma	To translate; translation	Tarjuma
Tarkao	To send; to send away by the employment	Tarkao

	of artifice so as not to convey the idea that one is being got rid of	
Tarkha	To threaten; to speak loudly and threateningly; violently; vehemently	Tarikha
Tartar	To tear; to rend; to crack; to split	Tartar
Tarwa (M)	Palm of the foot	Talwa
Tarware (+M) tarwair	A sword	Talwar
Tas	Playing cards	Tash
Tasbir (M)	Picture	Taswir
Taskao (M)	To knock	Kharkao
Tasla (+M)	A brass vessel used to cook in	Tasla
Tat (+M)	Sackcloth; gunny cloth	Tat
Tata (M)	Grandfather	Dada
Tatao	To warm; to heat; to stir up; to energize	Taona; ta dena
Tatbir; totbir	To take care of; to look after	Tadbir (to think about)
Tati (+M)	A screen; a shutter or a	Tati

	door of mating; branches &c.	
Tawa (+M)	A kind of flat earthenware vessel	Tawa
Tayo; thayo	To clap the hands	Tari
Te (K)	Then	Te
Teag	To leave; to abandon; to desert; to forsake; to quit; to abdicate; to give up	Teag
Tear	ready	tiar
Teh (K)	To bind; to fasten	Teh karna
Tehara (R)	Tomorrow	Dehara
Tej (+M)	Sharp; pungent; spirted; strong	Tez
Tejpat (+M)	A leaf used as spice	Tezpat
Tek	To live; survive; be living; stop; stay; to hinder; to obstruct	Tek (support)
Tekao (+M)	To bar; to obstruct; to prevent	Tok; tokna
Tekhar	Times	Tekhar

Tekhra tokhri	To squabble; to dispute	Turki-be-turki
Tekhrao	To repeat a question; to question or interrogate repeatedly	Duhrao
Tekhrar	To dispute; to altercate	Takrar
Tela; telalnu (R)	Under; below	Thala; tala
Tele (R)	Down; downstairs	Thele
Tele	Young lice	Leekh
Teli (+M)	Oilman	Teli
Teli (R)	Step-down	Thele
Teliga (R)	Cart; horse drawn buggy	Tanga
Tembe tira; tembe turi	Small; applied to children	Tabar
Tempa (M)	A short stick used for driving cattle; having a knob at one end	Tamba
Ten	To be pressed down by something lying on the top; to be caused to be pressed down	Tun; tun-na
Tenda bayar; Cenda bayar	A young buffalo with six teeth	Sanda

Tenda-dang	A contrivance for raising water from a well	Tendan
Teng (M)	To weave	Tanana
Tengo (M)	To carry on shoulder	Tengo
Tentha; thentha (M)	Small; mischivious	Laontha; tanta
Tep	Corner of a piece of cloth; state; position; gist	Tep; teep
Tepet	To block up; to close up; to stop up	Tepet (as in â€˜teep da band’)
Tera; teratera	Squinting; oblique eyed	Tera
Terel	The Indian Ebony tree	Dhraik; taraik
Tes	Imitative sound of the noise produced by anything brittle; snapping or clicking	Tes (wave of sharp pain)
Tese	Through; on account of; by reason of; owing to	Tese
Tesra	Third	Tesra
Tetan	Thirst; to be thirsty	Tareh; teriha
Tetang (M)	Thirst; to be thirsty	Tareh; terhaia

Tethor	Obstinate; heady; rude	Kethor
Thaatha (+M) thata	To make fun; to joke; to jest	Thaatha
Thaba thobo; thabu	In cluster	Thaba
Thabri (M)	To slap	Thapar
Thag (+M) thakbaj	To deceive; to oppose; to swindle	Thag
Thagal; thaglao; thangal thangal	To bite as a snake by darting	Dang
Thagar (R)	King; chieftain; headman; ruler	Thakar
Thagrani (R)	Queen; female ruler; wife of Thakar	Thakrani
Thah	Bottom; to fathom	Thao; theh
Thahrao (M)	To settle; to decide; to appoint	Thahrao
Thahri	Slowly; gently; disjointedly	Thari; tharna
Thai (R)	And; also	Te
Thai; thao	A place; to place; to give in marriage	Thaon
Thaili; thaila (M)	A bag	Thaili; thaila
Thain (K)	To weave; knit; district;	Than

	direction	
Thakao (+M)	To be tired; to be exhausted	Thakao
Thake thak	In heaps; in bands	Thaka thak
Thaket; Theket	To come into contact with and be brought to a stop	Thak
Thakna	Cheat	Thagna
Thakna; thakao; Thakua	To deceive; to cheat	Thagna
Thakrao	To upbraid; to wit; to threaten; bring up an old matter	Takrao
Thakur	supreme being;the	thakur
Thakur; murmur thakur	The supreme being	Thakur
Thali	To sink; as in bog; quicksand; mud &c.	Thale
Tham	A prop; a pier; as of a bridge	Tham
Thambhao	To settle; to remain; to be firm; to be permanent	Thuk ke
Thamkao (M)	To be stopped	Thamao (tham pao; thal pao)

Than (+M)	A piece or web of cloth	Than
Than (R)	Location; place; scene; spot; site	Than
Than; thani; thanit	Place	Than
Thana (+M)	Police station	Thana
Thanda	Cold; to make cool; to comfort; to assuage; to refresh	Thanda
Thanedar (+M)	The person in charge of a police station	Thanedar
Thanel	Udder	Than
Thao (M)	Place; spot	Than
Thao ku thao	In some places and not in others	Than kuthan
Thap	A kind of preforming doll which the performer causes to clap its hands producing a sound resembling to thap; thap	Thap
Thapa (+K) thap	To slap; to hit; to beat lightly	Thapar marna
Thapa thopo	To slap each other	Thaparo thapri
Thapi (M)	A small	Thapi

	wooden mallet; used by brick masons	
Thapna	Erect	Thapna
Thapna; thapni	To erect; to set up; as an idol	Thapna; thapni
Thapo thapo; thapre	To pat	Thapkana; thapki dena
Thar (K)	To pierce with a thistle or prick; to feel hurt	Phar; phat
Thar thar; tharatharao (+M)	To shake; to tremble	Thar thar
Thar	A line; a row; in lines; in rows	Thar
Thara; thari (+M)	A brass plate used to eat from	Thal; thali
Thasao	To do for; used in threats; to mix by kneading; to press clay into a crack of a wall; floor &c.	Thasao; dhasao
That thot	Stammering; flatteringly; to stammer; to falter in speech	Thathlana
Thatera (M)	Brassware	Thathera

	dealer	
Thauka (+M)	The whole piece as opposed a part; right; proper; exact; true	Thukwan
Thaura	To assemble; to gather together	Thara
Thawi	To reside; to lodge; to abide	Thahrna
Thekao (M)	To be steady	Tekao
Thekra	A wooden bell tied to the neck of a cow or bullock	
Thela gadi	A carriage pushed by men	Thela
Thela thili; thelao; thelepaese	To push or shove; as in crowds	Thela thili
Thela	To push; to shove	Thela
Thendga	A staff; a club; a cudgel	Dang
Thepo (+M)	To defy; to show the thumb as a defaince	Thenga
Ther	To brag; to bluster; to talk big	Phar
Thesao (M)	To push; to	Thesao; dhesao

	throng	
Thethor; tethor	Obstinate; heady; rude	Chichora
Thik thak (+M)	Exact; right; correct; accurate	Thik thak
Thik	Correct	Thik
Thika	Contract	Theka
Thikadar (+M)	A contractor	Thikadar
Thikan	To find out; to trace; to detect; to place; to fix; to settle; to ascertain	Tikan (tuka is derivation)
Thipi (M)	A cork	Thipi
Tho	To spit; to expectorate; spittle	Tho
Thobla; thopa; thube;thube thube	A cluster; in clusters	Thaba (it may be thoba)
Thokao (+M)	To hammer	Thokna
Thokar (M)	Collision	Thokar (Pb. where water collides with some structure)
Thoke thok (+M)	In heaps; in bound &c.; crowd	Thok
Thor (M)	To understand; to remember; to know	Thoh (pata thoh huna)
Thora; thora bahut (+M)	A little	Thora
Thos (M)	To end; to	Thus (thus huna)

	come to an end	
Thotha	Very; applied to obesity	Thotha
Thotha; totha; thothia	Having a defect in speech	Thatha
Thothkao (M)	To peck; to pierce	Thoko
Thothra (M)	A stammerer	Thatha
Thotna (M)	Mouth	Thothna
Thu (M)	To spit	Thu
Thubri	To adhere to; to stick to; as clay to boots; grass; weeds &c. to plough	Chambri
Thud (R)	Milk	Dudh
Thukau; dil thukau	To be resolute; to be dtermind	Thukwan
Thum	A boundary mark; post; pillar	Tham
Thupi	A small woodem mallet used mainly to beat plaster	Thapi
Thus marte	With a snap or crack	Dhus marke
Thuv (R)	Smoke	Dhuwan
Ti (M)	Hand; forearm; contest; power	Tali; hath

Tiag; teag (+M)	To give up; forsake	Teag
Tiar; tear (M)	To make; to prepare	Tiar
Tibhi; tighi	To prop up by means of a post with a V shaped head	Tibhi
Tice	To be equal to; to resemble; to be similar; to be like	Tice (like in tic button)
Tij; cij	A thing; an article; goods	Ciz
Tika (+M)	To vaccinate	Tika
Tika	Inoculation	Tika
Tika; tikak	To make a mark on the forehead	Tika
Tikau (+M)	To remain; to last; to be stable; to live; to survive	Tikau
Tikha tikhi	Painful; as a boil; hot and painful	Tikha tikhi
Tikis; tikit (+M) tikas; tikli	A ticket; an adhesive stamp	Tikit
Til	The plant which yields Sesame oil	
Tilak (+M)	A mark which Hindus make on their	Tilak

	forehead with colored earths or unguents	
Tilha (+M)	A small rising ground; a mound	Tila
Tilha	Mound	Tilla
Tin	Three	Tin
Tin	Three	Tin
Ting (M)	To kindle fire; to insert fuel wood in order to kindle fire	Ting
Tipa (M)	A drop	Tupka
Tipan (M)	To sew	Tipan; topa-laona
Tiras; tirasa	Thirst	Tirha
Tirin taran; taran tiriu	To speak angrily; to speak loudly	Toon tran
Tiro (R)	Your	Tera
Tirsul	A trident; or three pronged lance	Tirchul
Tisra; tisri	One eyed; blind in one eye (male; female)	Tira; tiri
Tito	Bitter; pungent; acrid	Khata
Tiyatra (R)	See	Yatra
Toa	Female breasts	Than

Tobe; tobe nahin (+M)	Then	Tabi; tain
Tod (M)	To knock the foot against an obstacle	Thuda
Toda	The sharp point of a wooden plough in which the share is fixed	Chau
Toe	A part of the female organ	Titi
Toe; tone (M)	To break; to fracture	Toe (ditches); tutna
Tok	A large pestle; used to husk and clean grain.	Mola (used in ukhli)
Tokor	Jinglingly	Tokor
Tola (+M)	A weight almost equal to half an ounce	Tola
Tolao	Assess	Tolo
Tolob; tolop	Pay; wages	Talab (demand)
Tomba	To accumulate; as water in hollow	Tobah
Tomosak	A note of hand; bond; obligation	Tomosak
Tomtombao	To the brim; full to the brim	
Toncok	A fault; a	Bholcook

	defect; doubt	
Tondehi	To investigate; to enquire into	Tandahi (with full body force)
Tonge	To join; to unite; to join end to end	Tang
Tonkhha	Wages; salary	Tankha
Tono (R)	Tone; sound	Dhun; tan
Tonta	To lack; to be in need of; to be scarce	Tot
Top (M)	A canon	Top
Top; topok	A drop	Tupka
Topa	To burry; to cover over	Topa
Topar	To cover; to blindfold	Khope
Tope	To cut; to clip	Tope (to sew)
Tora (+M)	A bag for holding money carried bound round the waist underneath the clothing	Tora (Any bag carrying goods)
Toraju	Scales	Torazo
Torao	To pause; as between the ending of one song and the beginning of another; to pause in the	Tora

	execution of a dance	
Toras	To be troubled; to be frightened	Taras (tarah is derivation)
Torphar	Unreservedly; keeping nothing back	Monh-phat; torphar (wrecking)
Tota (M)	To break; to break by plucking	Tota
Tota	A cartridge	Tota
Tothna	Snout	Thuthna
Totko	A wooden bell hung round a cow or bullock's neck	Talli
Totra	Having a defect in speech	Totla
Trad (R)	Admonish; warn	Trandna; trahna
Trash (R)	Alarm; apprehension; fear; horror; terror	Tras (tras tras kanbna)
Tristo (R)	Dejected; depressed; sad; lonely; pathetic	Taris (sympathy)
Triwar (R)	Three times	Tin-war
Trush (R)	Thirst; drought	Treh
Tu (R)	You	Tu
Tukra	piece	tukra

Tukra; tukri	A piece; a fraction; bits; broken pieces	Tukra; tukri
Tukri	A kind of bamboo basket	Tukri (basket)
Tul (+M)	To lift; to raise	Tul
Tula (+M) tulandani	Scales; a balance; to weigh	Tula
Tulan; tulni	To compare; to copy; to collect; to weigh	Tulna
Tulni (M)	One who lifts or carry	Tulni
Tulsi (+M)	A plant carefully tended and worshipped; basil plant	Tulsi
Tumba	Gourd	Tumba
Tumen (R)	You; yourselves	Tusin
Tun ghuri	A little time	Tin ghari
Tun tun	Tight; tense	Tun tun
Tun	A little	Tun
Tunda; tundu	To prod; to poke at as with a stick	Tungna
Tundi	The point where the shafts of a bullock cart	

	unite; and where yoke is attached	
Tungau (+M)	To snip off with the fingers	Tungna
Tunti lota	A lota with a spout	Tunti lota
Tunti	To spurt; to issue with force from a small opening;	
Tupi; tupri (+M)	A percussion cap	Topi
Tupo (R)	Toupee	Topi
Tupri	Cap	Topi
Tur	The roller on which the cloth is rolled by the weaver as he weaves	Tur
Tura; turi	A little	Thora; thori
Turat; turte	Immediately; instantly; at once; without delay	Turat

Turia	Age	Turia
Turkal	Light sleeping; easily awakened	Pb. Tarkalan is the time before sunset and long after mid-noon)
Turuk (+M)	Muslim cavalry	Turk (every foreign born Muslim was called Turk by the indigenous Indians)
Tusa (+M)	A bud; a leaf bud; a shoot; the tip; to break with the fingers	Tusa (Pb. food is called tusa when referring disparagingly)
Tut	Mulberry	Tut
Tut; tuti (+M)	Loss; to suffer loss or damage	Tut
Tuta bhanga (+M)	Fragments; pieces; broken; cracked	Tuta bhajia
Tutau	To be broken; to be fractured	Tutna
	U	
Ucharan (M)	To pronounce	Ucaran
Udam (+M)	Work; trade; profession	Udam
Udan	To fly; to squander; to waist; to dissipate	Udan
Udas (+M)	To look distressed; sorrowful	Udas
Udau	Fly	Udana
Udhar (+M)	On credit; not	Udhar

	paying readily	
Udhar	Credit	Udhar
Udhiau	To boil over	Udhiana (pomp and show)
Udhin	Submission; subjection; dependence	Udhin
Udia; udi	Flying away; carried away by the wind	Udia; udi
Udrau	To go on the impulse of the moment	Udari marna
Ughar; ughran	To uncover; to expose	Ughar
Uh (M)	An exclamation of pain	Uh
Ujar (+M)	To lay waste; to desolate; to ruin; to devastate; deserted	Ujar
Ujar major (M)	To object; objection	Uzar
Ujhlau	To pour ot	Uchlao
Ujur mujur	To petition; to make application	Arzi
Ukharao	Eradicate	Ukhar
Ukhrao	To pluck up; to be rooted up	Ukharao
Ukhu pukhu	Stiffing; stuffy	Uchu
Ukhur	A large wooden mortar in which rice and other grains are husked; cleaned or made into	Ukhli

	flour	
Ukil (+M)	A pleader; an advocate	Wakil
Ukilatnama	Power of attorney	Wakilnama
Ular (+M)	To persuade; to induce; to heavily load a cart on one side as to cause the other side to rise up	Ular
Ulat Pulat	Topsy Turvy	Ulat Palat
Ulat palat; ulat pulat; ulta palta (+M)	Upside down; topsy turvy	Ulat pulat
Ulta ulti	To turn from side to side	Ulta ulti
Ulta; ultao (+M) Ulti-pulti	Reverse; opposite;	Ulta; ultao
Ulti	The reverse of what is known to be right	Ulti) vomiting)
Uláºi	To vomit	Ulti
Umadha jote	The thong which binds to the plough beam	
Umar (+M)	Age	Umar
Umar	Age	Umar
Umas	Lustful; under the sway of animal appetite.	Umas
Umdhum	With all haste; full drive; full swing	Udhum
Umi (M)	To become public; to spread; as a rumor	Dhumi

Unt (+M)	Camel	Unt
Upai	To make effort; to endeavor; to strive	Upai (to correct the fault)
Upar	On; above; upon	Upar
Upas (+M)	To fast	Upas; roza
Uphad	Disaster; distress; calamity	Aphat
Upja; upjau; upjan; upjon (+M) upjao	Crops; produce of the soil; to grow; the yield of a crop	Upja
Upra upri	Struggle	Upra upri
Upria	Strange; unknown	Opra
Uralia	One who incites; indues; allure	Uralia; urali (waris Shah uses the word as yaroliye)
Uran	To destroy; To lay waste; to devastate	Weran
Usar (M)	To complete	Usar
Uskur; uchkao (M)	To incite; to stir	Uchkal
Usul	High; lofty; tall	
Ut	Camel	Unth
Utar	The north	Utar
Uthau (+M)	To raise; to break up camp; to leave a place	Uthau
Utkao patkau	To turn over; as soil	Paltau
Utkao	To raise or force with leaver	Utkao
Utrau	To copy; to translate	Utrau
Utu dhutu	To do with might	Ut

	and main	
Uá¸áºįu	To fly	Udna; udaro
	V	
Va (R)	Yes	Va (some Pb. dialects use va instead of ha or he)
Va	Or	Va
Vakil (R)	Criticize; find fault; groan; moan	Vakil (pleader) 3
Vero; verya (R)	Cousin	Ver (brother)
Vi (R)	As	Vi (too)
Vucho (R)	Elevated; high; tall; loud	Uca
	W	
Wah (K)	A river; a stream	Wah
Wah bah (K)	A large river	Wah bah
Wakil	Advocate	Vakil
Wala (R)	Canyon; valley	Wadi
War (R)	Time (as in how many times)	War
Wara (R)	Female cousin	War (chosen one to marry)
Warkai (R)	Somewhere; wherever	Kete
Waro (R)	Male cousin	
Wast; was (R)	Hand	Hath
Wo (R)	He; it	Wo
Won (R)	They	Uhnan
Wor (R)	Or	Hor
Worraniya	Ploughed field; cultivated area	Wahan; wahi
Wudar (R)	Door; entrance	Dar; dwar

Wuzhu (R)	Cleant; neat	Wuzhu
	X	
Xer (R)	Ass; donkey	Khar; khota
Xordo (R)	Small; little	Khurad
	Y	
Yad	Memory	Yad
Yag (R)	Fire; light	Jalna; jgana
Yakh; yak	Eye	Akh
Yekh (R)	One	Ik
Yilo (R)	Heart	Dil
Ynjri (K)	A chain	Zanjir
Yugil (R)	Yoke (oxon)	Yug; juge
Yugo (R)	Neck yoke (for an ox)	Jula
	Z	
Zhal (R)	Flow; go; run	Jhal (as of water)
Zhuli; zhuvli (R)	Female; woman; wife	Zal
Zhuto (R)	Pair	Jut
Zhuv (R)	Louse	Jun
Zor (R)	Power; strength; vigor	Zor
Zorales (R)	Hard; strongly	Zordar
	Some More Words	
adhi	To reduce	adhi
badla	recompense	badla

bora; bosta	sack	bora; basta
ekrar;ikrar	promise	ikrar
jit	Victory	Jit
jora	pair	jora
karon;samjhao;sabab;	reason	karan; sabab
kharid	purchase	kharid
maldar	proprietor	maldar
met	To say; to tell	Met; mat (Pb. advice)
misil;nathi	record;of	misil;nathi
nala	ravine	nala
oro (M)	And; again	Aur
raj	reign;to	raj
renglec	Sharpley; graceful; handsome	Rangela
tokrar	reiterate	takrar